The Hypocrisy of Democracy

How the American Dream Became a Black American Nightmare

Rashaad Singleton

Rashaad Singleton

Dedication

To my mother, father, my brother Don and to my dear grandmother Addie Mae Hughes, who would never let me go to sleep before praying to God. I love you all.

CONTENTS

Pr face

In the year 2019, racism is thick as it's ever been. Why can't America bury this disease? Maybe it's because it refuses to deal with it. If a sick person ignores their illness instead of treating it, it will only manifest into something worse. Racism in America has never been treated. The majority of America chooses to ignore racism rather than treating it like the mental illness that is. People would like to hope that it will just go away, but that's not what a disease does. A disease harbors and that's what racism has been allowed to do here. Just how people are conditioned to be racist, they must be conditioned to not be racist. One thing is for certain, racism comes in all forms: miseducation, job discrimination, police brutality, housing discrimination, lead water, and systemic incarceration—and that's just to name a few. However, there are people of every race who choose to stand up against racism and they should be applauded. It is not an easy task to challenge the very fabric of America. But some do.

People don't realize what's really going on in this country. There are a lot of things that are going on that are unjust. People aren't being held accountable. And that's something that needs to change. That's something that this country stands for: freedom, liberty and justice for all. – Colin Kaepernick[1]

---

[1] This is a transcript from 49ers quarterback Colin Kaepernick's media session on Sunday, 28th August, 2016.

Rashaad Singleton

Chapter 1: The Elephant in the Room

What is Independence Day to African-Americans? Surely, everyone knows our ancestors were still enslaved on July 4, 1776 and many years after that. Whose independence are we celebrating? Is it perhaps the independence of the very people who enslaved us? Yes, the independence of white Americans I suppose. By defeating the British, America would finally get a chance to have control over their own democracy.

The definition of democracy is the practice or principles of social equality. Without social equality, democracy does not exist. It is merely an illusion. Has America treated African-Americans with social equality? One would have to be delusional to think so. Unless you call kidnapping a nation and enslaving them for centuries while committing genocide against them "social equality." Is social equality the orchestration of black codes, Jim Crow Laws, and mass incarceration, all with no reparations? Certainly not. The United States is the only nation who enforced laws on its citizens to not read, the black citizens that is. No other people in the history of America and perhaps the world, had laws written up preventing them from reading. Laws were so corrupt, that even a white person could be put to death for teaching black slaves how to read. Now why would a government go through that much trouble to prevent a nation of people from educating themselves?

The answer is fear. White supremacists have always feared that if black Americans researched their history and remember who they used to be, the psychological chains would break and the economic power would shift. To add, if you claim to be intellectually dominant, which white supremacy does, then there is no need to suppress another's people intelligence. However, if an oppressor fears that the people he is oppressing is more intellectual than him, wouldn't he make it his business to "dumb them down"?

After coming to this realization, obvious questions begin to form. For example:

- Why doesn't the American education system teach where the slave ships came from?
- Why doesn't the American education system teach what the original language(s) of the African-Americans are?
- Why doesn't the American education system teach what African-Americans original names were?
- Why doesn't the American education system teach what kind of culture African-Americans had prior to the Transatlantic Slave Trade?

When you don't know who you used to be, you are susceptible to becoming anything that you're not. The American government knows all the history of African-Americans, but they will not release it or promote it. It's not fair to neglect the beautiful history of West Africa or the aboriginal roots of America. White supremacy is when white teachers have black and white students in a classroom and the white teachers only teach about the kingdoms of white people. From ancient Rome to Greece, to the kingdoms of England to American presidents, we hear about them all. However, when did we hear about the Mali Empire? Who mentioned the Songhai Empire? Who taught about the Kingdom of Yahudah? Who taught that some black people were in America before slavery? Who brought up the fact that many European scholars were only regurgitating the information that they had learned in Timbuktu, an African city that was the intellectual capital of the world? (Interestingly enough, when Americans want to express distance, they will fondly say, "from here to Timbuktu." Most have no knowledge of the actual city or what it contributed to the world. It is only known for mockery.) To ignore the Kingdoms of one people, but teach the Kingdoms of other people, while both people are in the classroom, should be criminal. To do that is creating a supremacist mindset for white Americans and purposefully trying to create an ignorant mindset for African-Americans.

Even if black America is not aware of their rich history, their oppressors are. However, the oppressor is never going to give the people that he is oppressing the solution. With that said, black Americans must eagerly begin to research their own history for themselves, because valuable information will not be given to us from the same people who stole it. They know how great we were and they know how great we will be again.

We must have a revolutionized conscious. It must first start with education and knowledge of self. Acquiring knowledge of self teaches you how to love yourself for who you are. Knowledge of self is not just understanding what your history is, but understanding your very purpose for existence. After black people begin to do this individually, we must then build the black family back up. Family relationships are the reason black communities strived for so long under the harshest of conditions. White supremacists eventually figured that out. In later chapters, we will discuss how the U.S government purposefully created chaos in the hopes of destroying black families. When we build up black families and create stronger black communities, we will be able to have full control of the black economy. We have 1.3 trillion dollars in spending power. Yet, who are we spending all of our money on? Everyone else, but ourselves. The Chinese get the black dollar, white people get the black dollar, Arabs get the black dollar, Indians get the black dollar, etc. Now if all these groups were supporting black businesses, then black Americans would feel more included in this democracy. However, which one of these cultural groups are overly supporting black businesses? The author has not seen that phenomenon.

Because of this unjust balance in social equality, it is imperative that black Americans begin to master group economics as other cultural groups have. It is insane for an oppressed people to complain about the group of people oppressing them while simultaneously spending all their money with them. When this is done, oppressed people are only financing their own oppression. This is not done intentionally, but rather it is conditioned. Since pre-school, we have been psychologically conditioned to serve and depend on white people. From writing a list to a white Santa Claus or closing our eyes and praying to a white image of Jesus. We have been programmed to believe that the things we really want in life, we must ask a white man. When black Americans seek justice and reparations for slavery, there is hardly a white man in sight.

This nation was born out of white supremacy. Land of the thieves and home of the slaves. You would think that 150 years after slavery, we could finally talk about the history before slavery. You would think that the information of our original names, culture, and language would be released. However, that is not the case. This education system in America is not even teaching us about where the slave ships came from, but they can tell you what a dinosaur had for lunch. Why is this truth being concealed from young energetic souls? Out of fear. It is the fear that young black minds will remember their true greatness before slavery. It is the fear that black Americans will rise up and overthrow the power system known as white supremacy. It is the fear that teaching African-Americans their real history will make their white classmates feel less important. White Americans did not and still do not want to live with the guilt that they enslaved a prestigious people who had kingdoms and universities, so they make conscious decisions to leave specific facts out. They distort our history in order to appease the feelings of our white classmates. Therefore, they teach that African-American history begins with slavery.

They don't teach that in 1452 Pope Nicholas V wrote Dum Diversas. This creed was an order from the Pope to the King of Spain to reduce all non-

Christians to perpetual slavery. European Christianity was obviously not practiced in Africa and America. The rulers of Europe saw that as a perfect opportunity to rob and exploit the continents of not just its resources, but its people also. Yet, the American educational system conveniently skips right over that. The United States only teaches African-Americans that their history started with the lash of the whip. They purposefully leave out facts to ensure that the descendants of slaves stay in confusion from generation to generation. This confusion is the reason some people suffer from self-hate or an identity crisis. Falsifying and neglecting history is the reason why white supremacy is able to flourish in America so freely. It's imperative that real history be revealed and no longer whispered about. For example, slavery had always been practiced by the conquerors of war, but for the first time in world history, with the signature of the Pope, the color of your skin alone could subject you into a lifetime of servitude. Coincidentally, forty years after the Pope signed Dum Diversas, Columbus arrived on American shores. Soon, a new nation would be born and bred out of genocide and slavery.

"I do not want to miss a good chance of getting us a slice of this magnificent African cake." –King Leopold II

Chapter 2: Before Slavery

American education picks and chooses what it wants to teach its citizens. Black students are forced to study white achievements and Asian achievements, but nothing is taught about African achievements. By not teaching a people their proper history, you are purposefully and willfully putting their mind in a box, and in all sincerity, it should be considered a crime. There is no mention of the Mali Empire. There was no mention of the Songhai Empire. There is no mention of Mansa Musa, a black king who was the richest man that has ever lived. There were no tests given to students teaching them about Timbuktu, which was known as the greatest intellectual capital of the world.

The only African thing America gives its black citizens is a water downed, white-washed version of Egypt that we all know is a lie. We know Arabs did not invade Egypt until 642. One thing about Egypt, it is extremely hot. For an ancient people to build pyramids, they would have to have dark skin pigmentation to even withstand the sun. The point is, the ancient Egyptians were undoubtedly black people. However, white supremacists do not want the world to know that black people are capable of such accomplishments. There is another reason why America does not want to teach about the ancient black Egyptians also. That's because on the other side of Egypt is Israel. Before the building of the Suez Canal in 1869, Israel was considered North East Africa. This led many people to argue that the Ancient Israelites had to be just another group of African people with their own culture and history. America teaches nothing about black Israelites. We are only taught to believe that one group of people are from Israel. However, it is clear that the same time the man-made Suez Canal was built, the term "Middle East" was also born. The Suez Canal was built to remap Israel out of Africa to make it seem like the idea of black people originating out of Israel was impossible. This caused confusion on a global scale and still does till this day. Mostly everyone forgot Israel was in fact North East Africa.

However, in 1970 Dr. Yosef Ben-Jochannan wrote the book *African Origins of the Major Western Religions.* In it he writes:

In North Africa, just before the period of Christianity's legal entry into Rome—due to Constantine "the Great's" conversion in the 4th century—there were many Hebrew (Jewish) "tribes" that are of indigenous African (the so-called "Negroes") origin. These African Jews, as all other Romanized-African of this era, were caught in a rebellion in Cyrene (Cyrenaica) during 115 C.E. against Roman imperialism and colonialism. This rebellion also marked the beginning of a mass Jewish migration southward into Soudan (Sudan or West Africa) along the way of the city Aer (Air) and into the countries of Futa Jalon and Senegal (Senegambia) which lie below the parabolic curve of the Niger River's most northern reaches, where the City of

Timbuktu (Timbuktu, Timbuctoo, etc.), Melle (Mali) presently stands.[2]

Millions of black Israelites migrated to West Africa because they were fleeing from Roman persecution. So you can imagine that local African tribes, who were established already, felt intruded upon and were not too happy to see millions of strangers wandering into their land, practicing their own culture and having their own laws. This is similar to what the Hispanic community goes through today in America, but extremely more hostile. The Israelites often had to hide their names or nationalities out of fear that they would be attacked. Eventually, many of them adopted the name Igbo, and they became known as the Igbo tribe (although there are different branches). Arabs would eventually invade Africa and enslave millions of these Israelites. This time is known as the "Sub-Saharan African Slave Trade."

One of the cruelest acts practiced by Arab enslavers was male castration. This was genetic genocide as it would make men unable to reproduce. It is estimated that over 20 million people were enslaved during the Sub-Saharan slave trade. Although it's rarely taught in the American education system, this time is critical to understand. As time passed on, Europe rose out of the Dark Ages and begins to seek more territories to control. By the time Europeans decided to invade Africa, it had already

---

[2] Ben-Jochannan, Yosef A. A. *African Origins of the Major Western Religions*. Black Classic Press, 1991. 76.

been severely depleted and weakened by the Arab slave trade. Had it not been for the horrors and destruction of the Arab slave trade, black people of West Africa would have been able to resist the assault of the European Transatlantic Slave Trade. The remnant of wandering Israelites would be surrounded by never ending war and chaos. They had no land and no friends.

These Israelites, who had adopted the name Igbo, were eventually betrayed by local African tribes who did not want them encroaching on their land any longer, even though they had only been fleeing from captivity. Nevertheless, the migrating Israelites were attacked and sold to Europeans who were looking for free labor to build a new world. The society of America undoubtedly teaches that "black people sold black people" into slavery. However, "Black" is just a color and is not a nationality. More specifically, local tribes of West Africa were selling black Israelites who had entered their land while they were fleeing from captivity.

Emanuel Bowen was a British cartographer who drew up the "Negroland" map in 1747. Within this map, were the two primary ports for most of the entire Trans-Atlantic Trade. The names of these ports were the Gold Coast and the Slave Coast. Neither of these coasts is discussed in the American educational system. The Slave Coast lived up to its name and was the main port for the Transatlantic Slave Trade. "Slave Coast" was not it's only name though. Prior to being conquered, it was called the Kingdom of Judah and Emanuel Bowen made note of that. This information has not been touched in the American educational system mainly because it does not fit the paradigm that America tries to promote, which is that black Americans do not come from kingdoms, they come from jungles.

In 1771, the "Kingdom of Judah" was removed off the Negro Land Map by the same cartographer who had originally made the Negro Land Map. That was not by chance or coincidence. White supremacy was fully in effect, and their main goal was to white-wash and completely erase history in order to control the minds of the masses.

"And the Lord shall bring thee into Egypt again with ships, by the way whereof I spake unto thee, Thou shalt see it no more again: and there ye shall be sold unto your enemies for bondmen and bondwomen, and no man shall buy you." –Deuteronomy 28:68[3]

---

[3] *King James Version Bible*

So remember, to just say, "black people sold black people" is a vague and more importantly, an ignorant understanding of what happened. More specifically, local tribes of West Africa were selling black Israelites who had encroached on their land. Furthermore, it is essential to understand that slavery in Africa was more so, a form of indentured servitude. Another important aspect that needs to be understood is that most African Chiefs who were selling the Mbandu people of Angola and the Igbo tribe of West Africa, were only political puppets set up by European colonists. Many of the original African Chiefs were decapitated for resisting the slave trade. Many white teachers leave this out, however, this is crucial to understand.

In today's society, when someone mentions the name Ashanti, the first thing most black Americans will think about is the talented R&B star from Murder Inc. However, that name is much more deeper than that. The Ashanti Tribe is actually a Kingdom of people that live in Ghana, but they migrated there. Just as the Lemba Tribe do not originate in South Africa, just like the Igbo tribe do not originate in Nigeria, just like the Bantu people do not originate in Angola, the Ashanti Tribe do not originate in Ghana, each of these tribes migrated and many people believe it was from Israel. What's even most interesting is that they were the most sought out people in the Transatlantic Slave Trade.

In the Bible the Ashanti tribe are mentioned by name:
"1. This then was the lot of the tribe of the children of Judah by their families; even to the border of Edom

the wilderness of Zin southward was the uttermost part of the south coast.

42. Libnah, and Ether, and Ashan," - Joshua 15:42

The "ti" on the end of Ashanti simply means "The children of". Meaning all together, the children of Ashan, a family in the tribe of Judah. They were colonized by the British in the 1800's. However, the first thing the Europeans noticed, was that the Ashanti Tribe had strange customs compared to the local African tribes. For one, they circumcised their children on a certain day which was an Israelite custom. The majority of Hamites and Gentiles did not practice circumcision. So immediately they knew they were different. What solidified it was the high priest of the Ashanti Tribe. He wore a plate around his neck with 12 stones. This was identical to a scripture in the Bible.

"And thou shalt make the breastplate of judgment with cunning work; after the work of the ephod thou shalt make it; of gold, of blue, and of purple, and of scarlet, and of fine twined linen, shalt thou make it.

Foursquare it shall be being doubled; a span shall be the length thereof, and a span shall be the breadth thereof.

And thou shalt set in it settings of stones, even four rows of stones: the first row shall be a sardius, a topaz, and a carbuncle: this shall be the first row.

And the second row shall be an emerald, a sapphire, and a diamond.

And the third row a ligure, an agate, and an amethyst. And the fourth row a beryl, and an onyx, and a jasper: they shall be set in gold in their inclosings. And the stones shall be with the names of the children of Israel, twelve, according to their names, like the engravings of a signet; every one with his name shall they be according to the twelve tribes." - Exodus 28:15-21

Chapter 3: All Men are Created Equal

The "kidnapping of a nation" is not how we are taught to look at our voyage to America, but that is exactly what it was. Some of us were in America already and would be kidnapped and brought to Europe. Through the Transatlantic Slave Trade, millions of Africans and aboriginal Americans were kidnapped, enslaved and killed. Kidnapping and stealing would be the base of what would become the most powerful country that has ever existed. The history of African-Americans cannot start with the production of cotton. That would be a disservice to the ancestors. In West Africa, they were kidnapped from their homes and were told to march with no advance notice or no knowledge of where they were going. While being chained up from head to toe, they would march for miles and miles. The children did not need to be chained up because a child will always run behind their parents. Whenever they did stop and have breaks (which was not often), women and children were kidnapped to do the sexual will of the Europeans who were stealing them. Then when they got on the boat, they would be kidnapped in the middle of the day and night and raped again. If they survived that treacherous journey (which many did not), they would immediately be sold upon arrival to America. Babies would be kidnapped from mothers, wives would be kidnapped from husbands and sold to the highest bidder. They had been brought into land of their enemy for "bondsman and bondswoman". For 24 hours a day and 365 days a year, they were forced to do every will of their slave masters. No matter your age or gender, you was forced to work until a white man said "stop". Skeletons of slave children have revealed broken collar bones from over work which shows there is no line that white plantation owners would not cross in order to secure profit. From picking cotton to engineering, we did it all, and we received none of the fruits of our labor.

As soon as our ancestors arrived in America, there were always people willing to die for freedom contrary to all the "happy slaves" we see in movies. When they marched to slave ships in West Africa, some of them ran away. When they boarded the slave ships, many jumped over. When they arrived at the plantations, they ran away again. The notion that all slaves were happy and easy going about a lifetime of slavery is false. However, whatever measure they used to obtain freedom, the slave master was always willing to go further to keep them from reaching it.

Often when slaves ran away, neighbors were asked to help retrieve them. When this process failed, slave masters resorted to more organized tactics and develop a specialized unit called slave patrols. Slave patrols would be given good money to track slaves, who usually wouldn't get very far. People who specialized in slave patrols would start their own business and become slave catchers. Slave patrol was seen more as a good citizen's duty, but slave catching was big business. A normal day laborer usually only got one dollar a day, but a slave catcher could get paid fifty dollars for catching a slave and an extra five if he whipped him on sight.

Most slave catchers used bloodhound dogs to track slaves. The bloodhound dog was referred to as the "negro dog." U.S. president Zachary Taylor was a slave owner and he had many bloodhounds imported from Cuba solely to catch runaway slaves. It is said that many bloodhounds would be locked up at all times and only released to search black people escaping for freedom. This would condition the dog to think "kill" every time he was released. Bloodhounds have a super heightened sense of smell. When they would catch black people running for freedom, they would hardly leave any remains.

In other horrific circumstances, the vile injustices would continue. When slave mothers were off working in the fields, many of their new born babies were left unattended. They were vulnerable to white men who wanted to make some extra money. They would steal the new-born babies and take them to the swamps at night. In many cases, they would skin the baby alive. Then they would tie a rope in a knot around the neck of the baby and his torso. They would then throw the baby into the water and wait. Within minutes, the bleeding helpless child would be swallowed alive by alligators. The white men would then use a rope to pull the alligator in and then they would kill it by shooting it or hitting it on the head with a pickaxe. They would later sell the alligator skin for profit. Thousands of beautiful black children were stolen and killed just to make a few wallets and shoes. These injustices were beyond overwhelming for many of the slaves. Many would retaliate and fight back. Unfortunately, if one challenged the authority of the slave master (or any white person for that matter), that slave would be signing his own death warrant.

There is nothing under the sun that slave masters would not do to command complete obedience. Black masculinity always threatened white Americans and too much of it would not be tolerated. In some cases, they would take the strongest slave and bring him in front of the others on the plantation. Slave masters would have him tied down and he would rape them. Slave masters often used rape as means to emasculate slaves that they were threatened by. This was known as "breaking the buck" or "butt busting." This act of demonic humiliation was being done to keep the slaves in total control. In other cases, a slave's hands would be tied to a horse and his feet would be tied to another horse and he would be ripped in half at the command of a slave master. After experiencing this, black mothers would become overly protective over their boys and that trait is still passed down to this day.

"I grew up like a neglected weed—ignorant of liberty, having no experience of it." –Harriet Tubman

Chapter 4: After Slavery—Free to be Lynched

On Sept 22, 1862, Abraham Lincoln issued the Emancipation Proclamation. For over two hundred years, black Americans were forced to do the will of white Americans. The Emancipation was supposed to abolish slavery for the entire nation. Two were issued. The first was a warning to southern rebel states. It stated that if the southern states did not agree to the terms of the Emancipation, it would go into effect anyway. Within the Emancipation, it stated that all slaves were to be freed. When southern states did not concede to the agreement, Lincoln used the second Emancipation Proclamation which ultimately put it into effect. Slavery had been totally abolished by the federal government. Confederate soldiers would not give up their right to have slaves easily. The civil war lasted for almost four years. Robert E. Lee, general of the confederate army, surrendered to Ulysses S. Grant on April 9, 1865. The war was over and black people were free. Yet many black people in rural America would not hear this good news until much later.

In 1865, there were a total of 250,000 black people enslaved in Texas. General Lee surrendered in April, but slaves in Texas were not freed until June 19 of that year. This would become known as the true Independence Day for African-Americans, but unfortunately there were still black people being enslaved. Many plantation owners did not want to give up their "property." It is documented that the owners of Waterford Plantation in St. Charles Parish, Louisiana held African-Americans enslaved up until the 1960s. The American education system conveniently skips over this. History should be taught that directly after the Civil War, the "majority" of slaves were freed, but definitely not all.

Freed or not, no reparations would ever be given to the nation of African-Americans. Forty acres and a mule were promised to each slave. However, that promise till this day has gone unfulfilled. What is freedom to a person with no land who is constantly under the threat of tyranny? Oh, they were free alright. They were free to get lynched. They were free to the mercy of Mother Nature. They were free to be discriminated against when trying to get a job, and free to be discriminated against when trying to get a home. With no reparations, it was not freedom at all.

After slavery ended, white film producers purposely started pushing the false campaign that black men were dangerous and sexually aggressive. They wanted every white American to believe that the black man was a danger to society, especially the white woman. Yet it was not black men who had the reputation for raping white women during slavery. It was the white men who had the reputation of raping black women. Millions of rapes were committed by white American men and nobody wants to talk about it. There was a fear that free black men would want to retaliate for the sexual abuse committed against black women for over two hundred years. That could not have been further from the truth. Black people did not want revenge. They wanted freedom. They wanted land. They wanted peace. Nevertheless, black men would be lynched by the thousands. Black communities would be burned down because of false accusations made by white women. In some cases, entire families were hung on the same tree. When a black man would be lynched, thousands of people would show up in that town to watch as if it was a concert. It was their way to hold on to the past a little while longer. People would gather around and have picnics and take pictures with dismembered body parts. Fathers would put their sons on their shoulders to watch black men be tortured alive. No doubt in their mind, they were living the American dream.

Many lynchings, if not most, were based on false accusations. Despite being false, many prominent black communities were burned down to the ground because of this. However, through hard work and dedication, black people rose up against the odds and depended on one another to save each other. They were forced to trade and do business with each other and guess what? It worked. Black people begin to build lavish thriving communities all over America. The black dollar was being recycled within black communities and the rewards were great.

When we think of black communities today, the first thing that pops in most brothers' and sisters' heads is "ghettos" and "hoods." That was not the case a few decades ago. Slaves who had just got off the plantation became millionaires in just a few years. From Tulsa, Oklahoma to Rosewood, Florida, black people were building wonderful communities. Group economics had been mastered and black people understood the power of controlling the black dollar. There were black owned hotels, black owned taxi companies, and black owned grocery stores. To see a black community today that controls its own grocery stores, hotels, and taxis is like seeing a unicorn, practically impossible. People who were just locked up and confined to picking cotton had risen to great wealth in a very short period of time. That scared the hell out of white supremacists.

Almost every single thriving black community in the early 1900's was burned down to the ground at the hands of white supremacists. Thousands of innocent black lives were lost. Thousands of homes and businesses were destroyed. Thousands of acres were stolen. Looking back on it now, some scholars say it must have been an overwhelming, insecure feeling for white males to see people that they considered of lower class rise to great status so fast. The people that they had just owned as slaves a few years prior begin to acquire more wealth than they had. White males also begin to feel competition from black employees. People must understand. The slave masters never did the hard labor or the jobs that were too difficult. The slaves did, so who were the best with their hands? Black people. Who could work for long hours and not complain? Black people. Who had the intelligence to invent something without even being given the proper tools? Black people, black people, black people. Many white laborers no longer felt needed. They failed to compete with the work endurance of African-Americans. So what was white America's solution to this predicament? Violence.

On July 18, 1863 in Manhattan, New York, tensions boiled over. White males of mostly Irish descent had been agitated because the black work population was doubling in size. They were also upset at wealthy white men who were able to pay three hundred dollars to not go into the Civil War, but instead send a replacement. The lower white class was not happy about any of this. They got together in what was supposed to be just a protest for the war draft. However, as they moved through the communities, they got distracted. Their cause for protest completely changed. They begin to attack all the black people they encountered. Over 100 people would be killed. Many black homes and black businesses were burned to the ground. The rioters even took it upon themselves to burn down a children's orphanage, the Colored Orphan Asylum. It was one of the first ever orphanages for black children. With all the racial violence and lack of resources, one can only imagine how many black orphans there were in America at the time. The Colored Orphan Asylum housed over four hundred black children. White supremacists burned the building to the ground.

It did not take much for a lynch mob to enter a black community with the intentions of burning everything in it. Usually, all it had to be was a false accusation of a white woman. In Atlanta in 1906, a newspaper printed that four white women had been raped by black men. No rapes were ever proven. Nevertheless, the story was out and white men were enraged. Fifteen-thousand white men showed up in Atlanta roaming the streets, stabbing, beating, and killing all black people in sight. Black people were lynched from lamp-posts and pulled out of their vehicles and killed on sight. Many black homes and black businesses were burned to the ground. This lasted for two days.

In 1917, the Great Migration was underway. Black people from the south were fleeing north in great numbers after being exasperated from racial tyranny and discrimination. However, in some places such as East St. Louis, Missouri, their problems were just beginning. Two-thousand black people were fleeing into St. Louis every week. White people were furious about it. White men began to be nervous about job security. They felt threatened by the arrival of southern black workers who were just as skilled as they were, if not more. On top of that, it was rumored that black men were beginning to date white women and that was the straw that broke the camel's back. On May 28, 1917, three thousand white men took to the streets, beating and attacking every black person they could find. Over two hundred and fifty African-Americans were murdered. One of the rioters was quoted to say, "Southern negroes deserve a good lynching."

In 1919, the summer was given the title "Red Summer" for obvious reasons. There were violent events happening almost daily. Sometimes twice a day in different states. On July 21st in Norfolk, Virginia, a racist group of white people attacked the celebration of African-Americans who were coming home from World War I. White people were not accustomed to seeing black people celebrated and glorified. This made the white men there uncomfortable. On top of that was the fact that the black men being celebrated were making just as much money as they were, if not more. The black soldiers and families were attacked, six people were shot.

On July 27th, the unthinkable would occur. Public beaches such as Lake Michigan were segregated. Eugene Williams, a black child, swam in the part of the ocean that was supposed to be "white owned." White supremacists stoned Eugene and drowned him to death. A little child swam in the "white only" part of the lake and white supremacists took it upon themselves to brutally murder him. When news got back to the other black people in the community, outrage broke out and a white man was killed. White people would retaliate on the entire community. They burned down and destroyed hundreds of businesses and homes on the south side of Chicago. Thousands of black people were left homeless. It is said that over fifty black people lost their lives.

On August 30th, a white mob formed in Knoxville, Tennessee. A black man had been suspected of murdering a white woman and white people around the community were livid. A lynch mob attacked the County Jail in Knoxville and they freed sixteen white prisoners. That was not satisfying enough though. They wanted to destroy more. News of the successful black business district that was nearby had been circulating throughout the whole state. They wasted no time before marching for it. Once they reached it, they burned it down to the ground.

Many thriving black communities would end up in ashes just because of the mere accusation that a black man may have assaulted a white woman. The law is supposed to go by the code of "Innocent, until proven guilty." However, to the black community, it seems that the law is "guilty, until proven innocent." Back in the early 1900s, it was even worse. It was "if accused, guilty with the punishment of a swift execution." In most instances, these accusations were false. However, the ramifications of these lies would be very real.

In September in Omaha, Nebraska, a white woman accused Will Brown of raping her. A mob of ten thousand people formed and marched to the courthouse. They attacked it and set it on fire. They demanded to have Will Brown. They kidnapped and lynched him. That was not enough though. They burned his body and stood around him like it was a campfire. On top of that, they burned down many black stores and homes. Take notice, whenever white people used to form in these lynch mobs, their priority was not just to kill someone, but to disrupt the entire black economy by attacking and destroying their businesses.

In Elaine, Arkansas, on September 30th, all hell would break loose. Unlike many racial riots, this tragedy would not be initiated with a false accusation. A group of black sharecroppers decided to have a work meeting and discuss their overly low wages. The white planters that were there did not like the idea of their black sharecroppers getting together and talking about business. The white planters decided to confront them. One white man was shot to death and another wounded. A militia formed immediately and attacked. It is said that nearly two hundred and fifty black people lost their life. The courts tried seventy-nine black people. Each one was found guilty. Twelve were sentenced to death. Some of the prison terms were up to twenty-one years. The white planters had won. Instead of paying pennies for sharecropping, they now had inmates who they could force to work for free.

In 1921, there was a black city making national headlines in Tulsa, Oklahoma. Nicknamed 'Black Wall Street", Greenwood was the home of black multi-millionaires. Only a few years out of slavery, some black men were already owning oil companies. How often do we here about black people owning oil companies today? Not often, if ever. On the other hand, in Black Wall Street, there were several. Black Wall Street had over six hundred businesses. They had twenty-one churches, twenty-one restaurants, thirty grocery stores, two movie theaters, six private airplanes, one hospital, one bank, and their own school system. Almost all of this would end up in ashes because of the false accusations of another white woman. Dick Rowland, was a shoe-shiner in town. A white girl accused him of assaulting her in an elevator. Police took Rowland into custody. Quickly, rumors began to spread that Rowland might be in danger of getting lynched. The rumors turned out to be true. A white lynch mob formed outside the jail. Local black men armed themselves and rushed to the jail to provide support for the police in order to help protect Dick Rowland. The lynch mob told the black men to drop their weapons and the black men refused. A fight broke out. Ten white men died and two black men died. When the news of these deaths reached the community, white people came together in the thousands. They destroyed the entire community overnight. Ten thousand black people were left homeless. The most outrageous detail about the Black Wall Street Massacre is that law enforcement officials orchestrated air attacks on black residential neighborhoods. Many innocent black families were killed. Till this day, Black Wall Street is the only city in America to be attacked in the air by America.

In Rosewood, Florida, there had been peace for the most part. The town was home to many black Masons. They had successful businesses and a thriving community. However, once again, all of that would go up in smoke as soon as one white woman falsely accused a black drifter of sexually assaulting her. Mobs of lynch-men formed overnight and burned almost every structure in Rosewood. It is said that over one hundred and fifty black people lost their lives, but the number of deaths could be much more. It was practically "open season" on black people. Black men, women, and children were murdered on sight. Not one single arrest was ever made. Land was stolen and houses were looted. Many black people were left homeless and had to flee the city. The entire black community was abandoned in just a few days much like other black communities around the nation. We will never know the full potential of some of these early thriving communities, due to the destructiveness of white supremacists and the false accusations of white women.

"Knowledge makes a man unfit to be a slave." - Frederick Douglass

Chapter 5: Black Codes and Jim Crow

When white supremacists were not busy burning black communities to the ground literally, they were coming up with other crafty ways of destroying the black nation. They would use legislature and law to keep black Americans in perpetual servitude. For instance, there were the black codes. The black codes were a system of laws that were placed upon black Americans after the civil war to prevent them from obtaining any economic or social power. The black codes had already been used by "Free" states prior to the war. For example, in "Article 13" of Indiana's 1851 Constitution, it stated "No Negro or Mulatto shall come into, or settle in, the State, after the adoption of this Constitution." In Maryland, a black person had to have a license from a white person to do any business. In many towns and cities, black people were not allowed to own land. Imagine trying to build a life for you and your family and the federal government says, "No, you can't have land." Black Codes were sadistic and nothing more than a "Free pass" card to continue to oppress and kill black people.

One of the cruelest facts is that black women were dared to speak out against any abuse by white men. This was evident in Illinois. In Illinois, black women were not allowed to testify against white men who had raped them. There were many elements of tyranny that were included in the black codes. In many regions, black Americans were not permitted to read and write, assemble in groups, or practice free speech. Black people were even prohibited from owning guns. Can you imagine that? How difficult it must have been to live in an area with hateful white supremacists and you're commanded by law to not protect yourself. Does that sound like a democracy? Does that sound like land of the free? One would have to be absolutely in denial to think so.

In other cases, black people were not allowed to have alcohol. That's because black people having "too much fun" was frowned upon by the white society. If a black person was walking on a sidewalk and a white person was walking toward them, the black man, by law, was commanded to get off the sidewalk until the white person passed. This meant that even the lower class of white America could feel like a king or queen in the presence of black people. (That must have been nice.)

But none of that would compare to the Vagrancy laws. Black people were just freed. They could go and come as they pleased and that was a shocking reality for a lot of white Americans. In fact, that enraged some people, especially the "Ole Massa", who had hundreds of acres of land with no one to farm it. He had one priority and one priority only; he had to get black people back in the fields. How would that be possible though? Slavery was over. The government even had union troops checking on southern plantations to make sure no slavery was happening. So how do you get black people to willfully go back and work for the man who has been brutalizing them all their life? You don't. You can't. Unless the person is completely out of his natural mind. Therefore, they resorted to other methods. White people decided to criminalize black people on a national scale. Through media and mass propaganda, white supremacists painted the picture of a black man as a mean, aggressive, out-of-control savage. There would be no mentioning of the fact that we were the greatest inventors in the world. They drew cartoons of our lips bright red and overly big. They made us look like tap dancing clowns. They said we came from monkeys and did not have the same intellect as white people, despite the fact that the base of all European knowledge came from Africa. They said we were overly sexualized, despite the fact that white men had been raping our black women for centuries and permitted by law to do so. All of this was hypocrisy, of this so-called democracy.

Because of the despicable propaganda and negative media, black men and more importantly, black masculinity became symbolic with danger. Simultaneously as that was happening, black people were being discriminated in the job market nationally. A black man that was trying to do well for himself and get a good job would be met with signs on the front of white businesses that read "white only," or, "no niggers allowed." The only jobs that were overly available were sharecropping jobs. This is the game that white supremacy plays. As soon as we left the fields, they were devising up ways to get us back in the fields. Except they would not call black people slaves anymore. They would change that name to convicts and sharecroppers. They didn't care what the names were honestly, just as long as they were back into the fields. Back in the sun. Back working for "Massa." You could decline working in the fields as a sharecropper, but there were so many white people discriminating on jobs that black people were constantly under the threat of breaking Vagrancy laws. The Vagrancy laws basically said it was "illegal for black people to not have a job working for white people." One could not even consider himself an entrepreneur. You had to work for white people or you were going to jail to slave for white people; it was as simple as that. That was the options for most of our ancestors. Soon the prisons would begin to fill up by the thousands. From young black boys to old age men—the government found a way to get its slaves back.

The process of convict leasing began. Convict leasing allowed wardens to live like slave masters. They had free black labor and they were looking for business. Wardens began to set up business contracts with legitimate businesses and plantation owners. Prisoners would be forced to do various deeds of work, often it was the most dangerous jobs no one else wanted to do. Prisons become billion-dollar businesses because of the fact that it's rooted in convict leasing. In the days of slavery, black people were considered property. Killing a slave was never in the best interest of the slave master. However, in the early days of convict leasing, prisoners were just an expendable employee. If a black prisoner died, there were thousands ready to replace him. Many innocent black pre-teens and teens were physically worked to death. It was slavery, but the government didn't call it that. It was slavery by a new name and it was just the beginning.

The black codes were developed to control what newly freed slaves could and couldn't do. However, there was a similar, but separate system that would guarantee to minimize black people's influence and power entirely. They were called the Jim Crow Laws. Jim Crow was originally a character played by a white man dressed in black-face in the early 19th century around the 1830s. His purpose was to demean African-Americans while providing entertainment for the white masses. He used to wear overly red painted lips and dark black paint on his face. This was supposed to be his portrayal of African-Americans. Politicians took this racial slur and ran with it. They used the name to title their racial legislative assault on innocent black Americans. The main objective of the Jim Crow Laws was to suppress and eliminate the right for black people to vote or have any influence in their communities. In most places in the south, black people were forbidden to vote. By not allowing black American citizens to vote, the United States government was telling black people they had no power to change the society that they had been forced to live in. Not only would they be disrespected in the political realm, but the disrespect would continue in everyday society as well. Racist politicians would introduce "Separate, but equal" clauses to make sure the disenfranchisement of black people would continue. Black Americans would have to walk around reading signs on businesses such as "No Negroes Allowed," and, "We Serve Whites Only." What a horrible reality to live in. To be told that your business is not wanted because of the beautiful shade of melanin that God has blessed you with. It's like blind people wanting to kill people that can see.

Woodrow Wilson became the 28th president in 1913. He had been elected from New Jersey, but Wilson was raised in the south. He would bring some of those "Southern qualities" to the White House. One of his first acts of president was enforcing segregation in federal workplaces. This was a social genocide being enforced by the very government who had just "Freed the slaves". It was not freedom at all, it was an illusion of inclusion. However, it is through great pressure that diamonds are formed, and out of the oppression of black Americans, many militant black leaders would rise out of the chaos. Their powerful voices would shake white supremacy to the core and challenge the hypocrisies in this democracy.

Booker T. Washington was the prominent black leader in the early 20th century. He was an educator, orator, and presidential advisor. He was born into slavery and never knew his exact birth date, although it's estimated around 1856. When the Emancipation Proclamation was signed, Union troops arrived on Washington's plantation and told him and his family that they were free. Washington is quoted in saying in *Up from Slavery*:

I cannot recall a single instance during my childhood or early boyhood when our entire family sat down to the table together, and God's blessing was asked, and the family ate a meal in a civilized manner. On the plantation in Virginia, and even later, meals were gotten to the children very much as dumb animals get theirs. It was a piece of bread here

and a scrap of meat there. It was a cup of milk
at one time and some potatoes at another.[4]

Out of freedom, Washington focused the majority
of his life on education. He would put himself through
school at the Hampton Institute. He would later be
suggested to be the leader of the Tuskegee Normal
and Industrial Institute. The school opened July 4,
1881. That would evolve into the Tuskegee University
that we know today. Washington's ability to unite
black people and get them from planning to acting
was unmatched. The school initially started in a
church that had an open space. As time went on,
Washington purchased a plantation where he began to
build the school from the ground up. Washington was
so motivating and inspirational, that he even got the
students to build the school themselves. By doing this,
they were able to learn trade and acquire a college
degree. This is important to note, because our
generation has put degrees before trade. However, our
ancestors focused on both. Not to mention, it's usually
the person who has the degree that works for the
person who has the trade.

After Washington published his book *Up from
Slavery* he gained national attention. It was about his
experience from being a slave to the leader of a
school. This book became so famous that the news of
its success even reached the Capitol. President
Theodore Roosevelt invited Washington to the White

---

[4] Washington, Robert T. *Up from Slavery*.
Unabridged Dover 1995. Originally Published
Doubleday, Page and Company, New York, 1901. 5.

House. No black person had ever been invited to the White House before that point. Many oppose the idea of a black man being invited to the White House, but Booker T. Washington's intellect could not be ignored. Washington fiercely believed that the way to combat racism was through education.

Booker T. Washington would have huge influence on many black people, but none more than a young man living in Jamaica by the name of Marcus Mosiah Garvey. Garvey was born Aug 17, 1887. His family lived comfortably in Jamaica considering the times. His father had a massive library and because of this, Marcus developed a huge passion for reading and learning. The most important thing he got out of those books was knowledge of self. As a teen, Marcus traveled to different regions around his home and that is where he began to feel the tensions that racism created. One day Garvey was traveling with a West Indian black man who told him of the horrors in his homeland from the impact of racism. Later that night, Garvey would have a vision that he needed to form a group to combat the oppressed life caused by white supremacy. He named the group Universal Negro Improvement Association (UNIA). Immediately, this became one of the most powerful black power groups ever assembled.

From Marcus Garvey's standpoint, along with many other black Americans, white Americans were incapable of living peacefully. The hatred that had been inbred in the majority of them for centuries was incurable, and he felt that in order to truly save black people, there had to be complete and utter separation. There could be no separation without land though and

Garvey understood that. Garvey worked out a strategy with the leaders of Liberia to make a massive exit for black Americans into Liberia. His plan was so flawless, that the United States government placed agents in his businesses such as his shipping company, the Black Star. These agents were there to literally destroy the work that Garvey had built. They purposely sabotaged the ships that would take black Americans to Liberia by tampering with the fuel. Nevertheless, no black person had ever been able to unite and get black people moving in such a way as Marcus Garvey did. Garvey's ability to mobilize millions of Americans in such a short period of time scared white supremacists to the bone. In 1925, the United States government deported Marcus Garvey without just cause. He would never return, but his work would never die.

"A people without the knowledge of their past history, origin and culture is like a tree without roots." –Marcus Garvey

Rashaad Singleton

Chapter 6: Ain't I a Man?

Black people were no longer asking for permission to be free, they were telling you. None more so than the Nation of Islam also known as the "NOI." This group of brothers were speaking like no black Americans had ever spoke before. Led by Elijah Muhammad, this group of black people were independent and strongly against any oppression from white supremacists whatsoever. Elijah Muhammad instilled a sense of pride in black men that had never been seen before. He had the ability to turn any black person into a better version of themselves and into a self-loving black person. That was needed so much due to the fact as stated previously, white supremacists had worked very meticulously at making sure we hated ourselves. Under the leadership of Elijah Muhammad, black men that thought nothing of themselves were able to turn their life around and have a sense of worth. Malcolm X, one of Elijah Muhammad's greatest students, would be the perfect example of that.

Malcolm X's real name was Malcolm Little. He was born May 9, 1925 in Omaha, Nebraska. From the time Malcolm was young, he experienced racial terror. His mother and father were huge supporters of Marcus Garvey and were heavily involved in UNIA. Eventually, word got out about their involvement and hate groups set their house on fire. Malcolm's family moved to Wisconsin. Time went on and they found themselves surrounded by the white supremacists again. Malcolm X's family second home was also burned down. As if it couldn't get worse, Malcolm

X's father was later killed by white supremacists. Despite that entire trauma, Malcolm X excelled in school. That is until he told his teacher that he wanted to be a lawyer. The teacher's response was that being a lawyer was "no realistic goal for a nigger." He dropped out soon after that.

Malcolm X did minor jobs here and there and eventually found his way into crime, later being sentenced eight years in prison for breaking-and-entering and larceny. In prison, he was introduced to Islam and his life was changed forever.

Malcolm Little changed his name to Malcolm X, stating "My father didn't know his real name. My father got his name from his grandfather and he got his name from his grandfather and he got it from the slave master." One must admire the efforts of the Nation of Islam and other black liberation groups who boldly decided to strip themselves of their plantation names and instead have a name of their own choosing. What superheroes they must have seemed like to stand eye to eye with white supremacists and say, "not anymore."

Why should any of us keep the names of plantation owners, arguably the most demonic people that have ever walked the face of the earth? Malcolm X dared black people to love themselves enough to release every psychological chain that the white slave master had put on them. He knew it was important to have a name of your own and not a slave master's name. He also understood that the black skin was symbol of divinity and he wanted black people to know it too. Black people have never heard a black man say such things. Malcolm X would preach "do for self", a concept that taught black people to depend on one another and never depend on their oppressor.

However, unlike his peers, such as Dr. Martin Luther King Jr., Malcolm X did not condone non-violent protests. Malcolm X was telling black people to defend themselves at all costs. He was not a fan of sit-ins, demonstrations that black people would organize in order to force white businesses to serve them. Many people were abused in these sit-ins. White people would hit them, spit on them and even pour food on them. Even if the racist business did serve you, Malcolm X thought you would have to be crazy to consume it out of fear that they probably tampered with it. Malcolm X and the NOI approach were very different from King's, however the goal was the same. Liberation. Malcolm X and the Nation of Islam believed that if white people don't want you in their establishments, build your own. Problem solved. They, along with Marcus Garvey, believed that utter separation was crucial. Malcolm X was the definition of being black and unapologetic, and the government agencies hated him for it. They knew that his ability to awaken the spirit of black men and women was only gaining momentum and there was no limit to what he could achieve. It's alleged that the United States government worked with secret agents to orchestrate his assassination.

No, I'm not an American. I'm one of 22 million black people who are the victims of Americanism. One of the…victims of democracy, nothing but disguised hypocrisy. So I'm not standing here speaking to you as an American, or a patriot, or a flag-saluter, or a flag-waver–no, not I! I'm speaking as a victim of this American system. I don't see any American dream; I see an American nightmare! – Malcolm X[5]

While Malcolm X was putting a fire under black people living in the northeast, there was still all-out hell being unleashed in the rural south. Black people were still getting lynched and discriminated just because of their beautiful shade of melanin. The black population was growing and white people were furious about it. In some towns in Alabama, white hatred was a burning flame, but a hero would rise out of the ashes.

In March 1955, Claudette Colvin was sitting on a bus in Montgomery, Alabama. Due to Jim Crow laws, black passengers had to stand and give up their seats for white passengers, even though they were paying the same fee. A white man got on the bus and asked for Claudette's seat. Claudette boldly stared the white supremacist right in the face and refused. She was arrested for being a hero. Only nine months later on December 1st, a woman by the name of Rosa Parks would go through the same ordeal. She refused to give up her seat up to a white passenger and was arrested on the spot. That was it. The black community of Montgomery, Alabama had seen enough. Outrage broke out and a local preacher by the name Dr. Martin Luther King Jr. and the NAACP would lead a 385 day boycott against Montgomery public bus transportation. The economic loss was great and it

[5] *Speech in Cleveland, Ohio (April 3, 1964)*

forced the Montgomery bus transportation to ratify their guidelines and end segregation. It proved that white businesses depended on "black dollars" just as much as they did "white dollars."

Dr. Martin Luther King Jr. was constantly being attacked. His home was even bombed by racial hate groups in his community. However, that did nothing, but to expand his voice on a national scale. Dr. Martin Luther King Jr. became the face of civil rights. He would later lead a march to Washington and deliver his infamous "I Have a Dream" speech. His speech was about the beautiful possibilities of two races living peacefully with one another. "I have a dream that one day this nation will rise up and live out the true meaning of its creed: 'We hold these truths to be self-evident: that all men are created equal." His message of love and humanity touched millions around the world. His stance was unchallenged and his views were undebatable. The Civil Rights Act would be passed on July 2, 1964 allowing all black citizens the same and equal rights as white citizens. Dr. Martin Luther King Jr. was eventually awarded the Nobel Peace Prize on October 14th, for heroism and being the epitome of a humanitarian. Black people nationwide finally had the right to vote and it was because of the leadership and willingness of Dr. King.

However, Dr. King was still troubled. He knew that the right to vote was not enough after being oppressed and enslaved for centuries. Black Americans needed back what was stolen from them. They need their land and resources, not just an apology for slavery. Reparations were promised by

the United States after slavery, but it was never paid.
Dr. King became very focused on this grave injustice.
He organized a group called the Poor People's
Campaign. Their main objective was to force the
United States to make good on their promise and
provide aid for the poor communities that had been
disfranchised. Dr. King was getting ready to have
another march on Washington in 1968. He gave hints
about what his speech would be about. He no longer
just wanted to talk about voting. King is quoted in
saying, "we are coming for the check." The
reparations that were never given were the top priority
on King's agenda. Unfortunately, on April 4th, a few
days before that speech was about to take place, Dr.
Martin Luther King Jr. was assassinated. The man
who had just won the Nobel Peace Prize had been
shot by white supremacists. The fight for reparations
never gained the momentum that it would have under
Dr. King's leadership, and that's exactly what the
government wanted.

Black leaders were being killed left and right and
black communities continued to be harassed and
mistreated. There was one group that had had enough.
On the West Coast, The Black Panther Party rose on
the scene in 1966. It was founded by Bobby Seale and
Huey P. Newton. The group formed in order to
protect themselves from police officers who were
abusing and harassing the black community. They
formed armed citizen groups and carefully watched
the activities of white police officers in their
neighborhoods. They strongly promoted self-defense
and they even developed programs such as the "Free

Breakfast for Children," which was created to promote love and care within black communities. Many leaders, men and women would rise out of the Black Panther Party.

Kathleen Cleaver is a hero and was a prominent figure in the Black Panther Party. Beautiful and educated, Kathleen led a moral assault on the European standard of beauty. She expressed that black people were made perfect and did not need to conform to European beauty standards in order to appreciate themselves. Angela Davis was also an iconic figure in the Black Panther Party. Eloquent and assertive, Angela Davis sacrificed her teaching career in order to fight the oppression of black people. Angela Davis stood up for righteousness and justice for black Americans and because of that she was fired by Governor Reagan and the California Board of Regents. Angela Davis's bravery never wavered. She continued to fight against white supremacy and was a huge voice in prison reform. There were many other black leaders whose roots began out of the Black Panther Party. They promoted love, awareness and self-defense. For promoting self-defense and feeding impoverished children breakfasts, FBI Director J. Edgar Hoover called the Black Panther Party "the greatest threat to the internal security of the country."[6]

"...You can jail revolutionaries, but you can't jail the revolution." –Fred Hampton

---

[6]https://www.pbs.org/hueypnewton/people/people_ho over.html

Rashaad Singleton

Chapter 7: Systemic Mass incarceration

White supremacy was killing black leaders like it was a sport. Malcolm X, a huge leader in the Muslim movement had been assassinated. Dr. Martin Luther King Jr., a huge leader in the Christian movement, had been assassinated. Fred Hampton, the young leader of the Black Panther Party, was assassinated when he was killed by the police in his sleep. Many more black leaders were killed for their audacity to demand freedom. However, because of their sacrifices, black Americans could finally vote, and we must never forget that. For the first time, white supremacists had seen what the power of a united black nation can accomplish. Rumors soared that their biggest fear was Dr. Martin Luther King Jr. running for president. Black people would have voted for him without thinking and many whites as well. Dr. King and the Poor People's Campaign demanding reparations was enough for white supremacy to unleash all-out war on the black community. J. Edgar Hoover, head of FBI at the time is quoted in saying "we must prevent the rise of the black messiah." There was a fear that there would be another black man that would try to unite the people and dare demand reparations again. So, the government took it upon themselves to make sure that would never happen by the means of Systemic Mass Incarceration.

Take the black man out of the black home. That was the goal of white supremacy and they succeeded. That is clearly evident when it comes to the infamous presidency of Richard Nixon, who's known for his infamous "Watergate Scandal." New information reveals he was not too fond of black people at all. He began an assault on black communities under the mask of the "War on Drugs." This strategy orchestrated by the federal government has been an absolute failure and any social scientist will confirm that. It has created more tension and crime, not less. Nixon's domestic policy chief, John Ehrlichman is quoted in saying,

We knew we couldn't make it illegal to be either against the war or black, but by getting the public to associate the hippies with marijuana and blacks with heroin. And then criminalizing both heavily, we could disrupt those communities," Ehrlichman said. "We could arrest their leaders, raid their homes, break up their meetings, and vilify them night after night on the evening news. Did we know we were lying about the drugs? Of course we did.[7]

"Of course we did." So nonchalant about destroying the lives of millions. So nonchalant about committing genocide against people you're supposed to call "countrymen". So nonchalant about leaving millions of black babies fatherless and black women unprotected. "Of course we did," he said. From the time of Nixon, the United States would see unprecedented numbers of criminalized citizens. Half of them have always been black despite the fact that we are only supposedly 12% of this population. How

---

[7] https://www.cnn.com/2016/03/23/politics/john-ehrlichman-richard-nixon-drug-war-blacks-hippie/index.html

can we be 12% of the nation's population, but 50% of the prison population? That is not by chance or coincidence. It was orchestrated from the very top. That is not justice. That is the contradiction of justice. That is genocide.

Soon afterwards, Ronald Reagan would take presidency in 1981. Reagan had always been in the spotlight, because he was formerly a successful actor prior to becoming president. When he became president, he wanted to be known as a "Law and Order" president. That's interesting, especially since under his watch, the CIA funded drug cartels that funneled drugs into black communities. How does pure Columbian cocaine end up in the middle of the hood? Black people didn't own any planes. Ask yourself; how does pure uncut drugs from other countries end up on MLK Street in the middle of the hood? How do all these war like weapons find themselves in our communities? Who's putting them there? See there is a root to black on black crime, and that's white on black crime. Systematic incarceration is incarceration that is run by a system and is self-running. Black Americans have been targeted within this system and now they're being targeted more so than ever before. This is evident since drug use between black and white communities are similar in numbers, but the African-American conviction rate is more than double that of white people. African-American prison population soared like never before during the years of Reagan. Millions of families would be and still are destroyed by Reagan's "Law and Order" policies.

After Reagan, a new wave of assault would hit black communities, President George Bush. In his very first presidential address on Sept 5, 1989, Bush held up a bag of crack. He held it up and said, that drugs were "the greatest domestic threat facing our nation today." He vowed to fund state organizations to double down on drug offenders. That's what he was telling the nation. However, in reality he was saying he was going to lock up black people like no one had ever done before and the data supports that is exactly what happened. Many broken families would be the direct result of Bush's escalation of the war on drugs.

Black people needed a new political leader. They needed a party that understood their needs and circumstances. Then a white man came on TV one night and sang some Negro spirituals and played jazz on the saxophone. Black people were smitten. Bill Clinton would be the next president after Bush and black Americans got him there. He had the hearts of millions of black people. Even I can remember the love black people had for him when I was a child. He was smooth and charismatic and the black community adored him. One would think the feeling was mutual until, he introduced his Three Strike Rule. Under Bill Clinton's rule, if a person had already committed two serious crimes, he would get a minimum of twenty-five years for the third crime, regardless of what the crime was. I repeat, a minimum of twenty-five years. Those ramifications are still being felt in black communities till this day.

So the black community had two major issues. Drug usage and jail. The same white people that were funneling drugs in black communities were also locking black people up for using those drugs. Two of the more popular drugs of that time were crack and cocaine. Cocaine was considered the drug choice of white people and professionals. Crack was the drug of choice of black people because it was cheaper and easier to obtain. Chemically, they are practically the same, nevertheless law differentiated them greatly. By law, crack users were to be sentenced one-hundred times more than cocaine users. This one-hundred to one disparity once again gave white America free labor and gave black Americans broken communities.

Clinton in 1994, stated "Blacks are right to think something is terribly wrong...when there are more African-American men in our correction system than in our colleges; when almost one in three African-American men, in their twenties, are either in jail, on parole, or otherwise under the supervision of the criminal system. Nearly one in three."[8] His 1994 crime bill instructed the Sentencing Commission to investigate the disparity. They concluded, that the one-hundred to one crack cocaine to powder cocaine quantity ratio is a primary cause of the growing disparity between sentences for black and white federal defendants. Unfortunately, by the end of their report, the Republican Party had gained control of the House of Congress. They wrote up a bill that would overturn the Sentencing Commission report. If the report had been considered, and if certain people had humanity, the disparity would clearly have been

---

[8] http://www.cnn.com/US/9510/megamarch/10-16/clinton/update/transcript.html

modified. Nevertheless, two weeks after giving that heartfelt speech about how black people are right to think something is wrong, Clinton signed the Republican bill, perpetuating the disparity. He said that black Americans were right to feel something was wrong and then hypocritically signed a bill that would add to the wrongdoing. All he had to do was veto the bill and he didn't. Rev. Jesse Jackson is quoted in saying, "Clinton had the opportunity to, "with one stroke of your veto pen, to correct the most grievous racial injustice built into our legal system."[9] He chose not to. Today, one in three black men will be systematically incarcerated. And as you can see, it's not by chance or coincidence.

With the authorization of the U.S government, one in three black men will be incarcerated at least once in their lifetime. After they are freed, they are left with little to no options. Every job application they fill out, they have to admit that they have a criminal past. Because of that, many felons have a hard time finding work, which makes them susceptible to falling back into crime. When they are lucky enough to find a job, they are taxed on their salary, but they are not allowed to vote. That sounds like "taxation without representation." White Americans decided to wage war on Great Britain for that very offense. America won and gained its

---

[9] http://articles.baltimoresun.com/1995-10-31/news/1995304052_1_crack-cocaine-powder-cocaine-cocaine-crimes

independence while at the same time denying that same independence to black Americans.

Nevertheless, pressure makes diamonds. Out of oppression and injustice, some of the greatest geniuses the earth had ever known rose to great prominence. One outspoken historian was Dr. John Henrik Clarke. His vast knowledge of history and cultures was unmatched and he challenged the practical teachings of western scholars. His masterful book, *Christopher Columbus and the African Holocaust* goes into great depth about how Europe was able to build itself up from the dark ages by robbing Africa of its resources and its people. The book describes how Africa was prevented from reaching its true potential by European powers and how they still try to control the descendants of Africans today.

"If you expect the present-day school system to give history to you, you are dreaming. This, we have to do ourselves. The Chinese didn't go out in the world and beg people to teach Chinese studies or let them teach Chinese studies. The Japanese didn't do that either. People don't beg other people to restore their history; they do it themselves."[10] –Dr. John Henrik Clarke

A good colleague of Dr. John Henrik Clarke was Dr. Yosef Ben-Jochannan.

---

[10] Clarke, John Henrik. *Africans at the Crossroads*. Africa World Press. 1991. 19.

Known as "Dr. Ben." He would challenge the authenticity of European scholars. He was a great teacher of Egyptology and believed that the original people of the Nile Valley were indeed black. He spent his entire life providing facts to prove it. One theory of his shook the foundations of Europe. He claimed the original Israelite people of ancient times were black people. This would raise many questions that we will explore in later chapters. What is really admiring about Dr. Ben was his respect for the African woman. His work described how the African woman was the mother of all:

Without you, African mother, there would have been no us--African fathers, sons and daughters. Do we need to say any more African mothers, our own true goddesses! Let us praise you to the highest, telling the world about your righteousness. Let us tell the entire universe about your sacredness African woman. [11]

There had been many men and women willing to wage war for freedom. One person who often goes unnoticed is Dr. Frances Cress Welsing. Dr. Welsing was an Afrocentric psychiatrist. Her work was groundbreaking. After studying white Americans and black Americans carefully for years, she concluded that the base of white supremacy was fear. Not just

---

[11]https://www.goodreads.com/quotes/65396-without-you-african-mother-there-would-have-been-no-us--african

any fear though, it was the fear of genetic annihilation. She made the claim that the most dangerous weapon that the black man had was his penis. Why? Because through his genetic makeup, everything he produces will be "black." This would explain why Europeans were so fascinated with castrating black men during slavery and such was the case with Arabs during the sub-Saharan Slave Trade. She also was one of the first scholars to go into great detail about the benefits of melanin. Many black Americans were and are under the impression that their shade of brown is some kind of curse from God. This is the effects of being taught and educated by white supremacists. Dr. Frances Welsing also wrote a groundbreaking book called the *Isis Papers*. In Egyptology, Isis is believed to be an African goddess and sister of Osiris. Many believe it is not by chance that the name Isis is more known for being the name of a terrorist group today rather than the African goddess who bore the name first. It is perceived that this was done to keep people from studying African theology.

In the *Isis Papers*, Dr. Frances goes into great detail about the global genocide of Africans from European powers. While fighting white supremacy through scholarship and academia, Dr. Frances made sure that black Americans understood accountability as well. She knew that before we could ever unite and fight white supremacy, we first have to "learn" to love ourselves. We had been conditioned through media and false propaganda for years to hate ourselves. She beckoned for black people to love themselves how they were and promoted the idea that they were perfect in their natural state with no European influences.

The facts of our true identity are that we, as Black people, are persons whose dominant genetic and historic roots extend to Africa, 'the land of the Blacks.' Africa was the birthplace of humankind and that for many hundreds of centuries thereafter, Africans, meaning Black people, were in the forefront of all human progress. As John Henrik Clarke states, "It can be said with a strong degree of certainty that Africa had three Golden Ages. The first two reached their climax and were in decline before Europe as a functioning entity in human society was born." Black women and black men are the parents of the entire family of people—black, brown, red, yellow and white varieties.[12]

In the 80s and 90s, no group was more influential in promoting self-love and unity than the NOI. Led by Minister Farrakhan, the NOI would challenge all who denied black Americans dignity and freedom. Louis Farrakhan was a student of Malcolm X and was also under the direct leadership of Elijah Muhammad. On October 16, 1995, Farrakhan and the NOI led a Million Man March in Washington, D.C. Farrakhan implored black men to take back control of their communities and establish order back in the black

---

12

http://kemet1.weebly.com/uploads/6/4/6/5/6465360/the_isis_papers_-_francis_cress_welsing.pdf family. Because of his unapologetic approach to black unity and fighting white supremacy, Farrakhan was cast out by many white media outlets and even some black communities. I can remember that even in my own community, when I was a child, people described Farrakhan as too radical and too hostile. However, after gaining knowledge of self and consciousness, one can clearly see that Farrakhan is only passionate for his people that are being oppressed every single day. Nevertheless, if some people do not agree with the tone of Farrakhan, they have to admit that his tone does not compare to the aggression of white supremacy. In war, one cannot be nice and sweet on the battlefield. A person has to be assertive and confident or surely he or she will suffer the consequences.

One of Farrakhan's and the NOI's greatest achievement was a series of books called *The Secret Relationship between Blacks and Jews*. Within the book are the works of many Jewish scholars who confessed that Jewish people help financed the Transatlantic Slave Trade. Despite the fact the book consisted of mostly Jewish scholars, it was branded "Anti-Semitic" by mainstream media. It was contradicting because, once again, the book was based off of what Jewish people said about themselves. So that's the predicament of black Americans right now. We are not even allowed to point the finger at the people who played a huge part in the Trans-Atlantic Slave Trade without getting labeled "Anti-Semitic." However, one cannot be anti-Semitic against a people who are not Semitic.

For example, there used to be an ancient European kingdom called the Khazarian Empire. The Khazarian Empire was faced with two decisions. In order to prevent annihilation, they had to convert to Christianity that was under the control of Rome or Islam and rather than choosing one, they chose Judaism instead. The King ordered everyone in the kingdom to convert to Judaism. This adoption of Judaism was purely political—it was not about faith. The descendants of this empire are said to be the "Jewish" people that we know of today. Many Jewish scholars would agree with that, especially Arthur Koestler, who wrote the book *The 13th Tribe*. This book goes into great detail about the Khazarian Empire and who they are today. Koestler writes: "The bulk of modern Jewry is not of Palestinian, but of Caucasian origin," and, "Their ancestors came not from the Jordan but from the Volga, not from Canaan but from the Caucasus."[13] All in all, Farrakhan and the NOI's book, *The Secret Relationship between Blacks and Jews* is one of the most underrated books of all time because it is filled with the truth that many of our white educators failed to teach us. Farrakhan once said, "There really can be no peace without justice. There can be no justice without truth. And there can be no truth, unless someone rises up to tell you the truth."[14]

---

[13] http://www.fantompowa.info/13th%20Tribe.pdf

A student of Farrakhan was a strong brother by the name of Khalid Muhammad. If people thought Farrakhan and Malcolm X were unapologetic, they got a reality check when Khalid Muhammad spoke. Khalid Muhammad was a prominent leader in the NOI and he would tell you exactly how he felt at any given time. He had the ability to inspire the youth and the elderly with great enthusiasm. He later became the leader of the New Black Panther Party where he traveled the nation speaking up about the injustices that were happening non-stop. He was able to unite thousands at a time when he spoke on liberation and freedom. He knew that to be fully liberated, black Americans had to have knowledge of self. Khalid Muhammad believed that he as well as other black Americans were in fact the Israelites of the Bible. The media attacked him, just like they attack any black person who dares to make that claim. He as well as many truth speakers would be blackballed from major media networks. Nevertheless, Khalid Muhammad continued to be a champion for black Americans till the day of his unexpected death. Khalid Muhammad desperately wanted black Americans to stop depending solely on politics and crooked politicians to save them. He believed that black people needed to separate and unite in order to practice group economics and to build their own communities. He did not believe that republicans were interested in such things, nor smiling democrats. He was relentless

---

14

https://www.brainyquote.com/quotes/louis_farrakhan_206804

in telling black people to do for themselves and to not depend on the people who had enslaved us only a few decades ago.

"People saying, 'I'm with the Democratic Party, I'm with the Republican Party.' Fool you ain't even invited to the damn party." –Khalid Muhammad

The NOI would also produce another Master Teacher, by the name of Dr. Na'im Akbar. Akbar is an American psychologist who questioned the discrepancies and the fairness of the American education system. He wrote the book "Breaking the Psychological Chains of Slavery." He would be one of the first people to go into detail about the privileges of being white in America and the ramifications of not being white in America. He expressed how amazing it must be to grow up in a nation where they tell you that your God looks like you. How amazing it must be to see images of all the prophets and they look like you and even all the angels look like you. He asserted that it was a great privilege to grow up in a nation that made you always feel like you were divine. With his unmatched eloquence, Dr. Akbar would bring white supremacy to its knees through scholarship and facts, with quotes such as:

When young Black boys learn that there are no limits to our possibilities on the basketball courts, we create the athletic genius of Michael Jordan or Magic Johnson and in their genius, they recreate the game of basketball. When our young people know that there are no limits to their potential in the world of manufacturing, communication, physics, chemistry or the science of the human mind, then those same young Black minds who create dances on the dance floor or compose music on their bodies with the 'hand jive' will recreate these fields of human endeavor with the same incomparability.[15]

One of the most underrated black scholars of all time is Dr. Amos Wilson, an American psychiatrist. He wrote the book *The Blueprint for Black Power*. In the book, he urges black people to "do for self" and to not depend on white people for anything. He exposed that the American education system ignores the realities and circumstances of black America. He stated that any education that does not teach you what your original nationality is, is an education that will enslave you. One of his most defining statements was that the education in America was an education for servitude. Serving who? White supremacy. He also stated that any religion that did not tell you which nation you belong to is a religion for servitude. Today, with so many black Americans praying to a white Jesus with blond hair and blue eyes despite the fact that the Bible never described him that way, it seems that Amos Wilson's theory is incredibly true. Truth and justice is what Amos Wilson stood for. As he says:

---

[15] https://www.goodreads.com/quotes/25081-when-young-black-boys-learn-that-there-are-no-limits

Justice requires not only the ceasing and desisting of injustice but also requires either punishment or 'reparation for injuries and damages' inflicted for prior wrongdoing. The essence of justice is the redistribution of gains earned through the perpetration of injustice. If restitution is not made and reparations not instituted to compensate for prior injustices, those injustices are in effect rewarded. And the benefits of such rewards conferred on the perpetrators of injustice will continue to "draw interest," to be reinvested, and to be passed on to their children, who will use their inherited advantages to continue to exploit the children of the victims of the injustices of their ancestors. Consequently, injustice and inequality will be maintained across the generations as will their deleterious social, economic, and political outcomes.[16]

It seems to me that white Americans have many conversations about what black Americans need to do to improve their circumstances. However, hardly any of those conversations begin or end with reparations, and no one understood this more than Dr. Randall Robinson. Dr. Robinson was a law student of Harvard University and he was known for his radical pursuits of justice. He was a major activist in the anti-Apartheid movement in South Africa. He also played an incredible role in restoring democracy in Haiti. In

---

[16]   https://www.goodreads.com/quotes/1313544-justice-requires-not-only-the-ceasing-and-desisting-of-injustice

2001, Robinson wrote the book, *The Debt: What America Owes to Blacks*. In the book, he explains how white supremacy robbed us of everything and gave us back nothing, but said, "we are equal." Because of this blatant neglect from both political parties on the issue of the unpaid reparations, white supremacy was able to flourish freely without wearing white hoods. Randall Robinson's book was highly praised because it tackled a controversial topic so eloquently. However, skeptics still claim, as so many like to do, that his cry for justice and liberation was "reverse racism."

No race, no ethnic or religious group, has suffered so much over so long a span as blacks have, and do still, at the hands of those who benefited, with the connivance of the United States government, from slavery and the century of legalized American racial hostility that followed it. It is a miracle that the victims–weary dark souls long shorn of a venerable and ancient identity–have survived at all, stymied as they are by the blocked roads to economic equality.[17]
–Dr. Randall Robinson

Another champion for reparations is Dr. Claud Anderson. Dr. Anderson wrote the book *"Black Labor, White Wealth."* In the book, he goes into great detail about how white supremacy has been able to keep their power because of the injustices they did economically to get that power. He explained that

---

[17] https://fog.ccsf.edu/~abair/thedebt.pdf

black people needed to change how they spend their money. He specified how white people, Asian people, and other culture groups rarely support black businesses. Yet surprisingly, black people support everyone's businesses except their own. He explained that the dollar circulates six to seven times before it leaves Latino communities. In white communities, the dollar circulates eight to twelve times. In Asian and Arab communities, the dollar circulates thirteen to fourteen times. In the Jewish community, the dollar bounces twenty times before it leaves. However, with the black community, the dollar does not bounce one single time. His work made it clear, since the American government refuses to pay or even acknowledge reparations, black people had to change the way they spend their money in order to not finance their own oppression. By doing this, we are able to take power rather than begging for it. His vast knowledge of economics painted clear pictures for the black community. He says in his book *PowerNomics®:*

Racism is wealth—and power-based competitive relationship between Blacks and non-Blacks. The sole purpose of racism is to support and ensure that the White majority and its ethnic subgroups continue to dominate and use Blacks as a means to produce wealth and power…True racism exists only when one group holds a disproportionate share of wealth and power over another group, then uses those resources

*to marginalize, exploit, exclude and subordinate the
weaker group.*[18]

Many black scholars questioned why black
Americans failed to practice group economics. Some
leaders came out said it's because African-Americans
have been severely traumatized without even knowing
it. Dr. Joy DeGruy, an American psychiatrist, and
author of *Post Traumatic Slave Syndrome* expresses
how the trauma that our ancestors endured still plays a
part in the relationships that we have with each other
today. Let's not forget about white people as well. We
never talk about how slavery conditioned them to be
racist and feel superior. After slavery, did this
government set up institutions to teach white people,
how not to be racist? Absolutely not. Does racism just
go away for white people? Absolutely not. Not only
that, but white supremacy conditioned black people to
self-hate themselves, does self-hate just go away? No.
If one is conditioned to be negative, they have to be
reconditioned to be positive.

*Although slavery has long been a part of human
history, American chattel slavery represents a case of
human trauma incomparable in scope, duration and*

---

[18] Anderson, Claud. *PowerNomics®: the National
Plan to Empower Black America.* PowerNomics Corp.
of America, 2001.

consequence to any other incidence of human enslavement.[19] –Dr. Joy DeGruy

Europeans control the history, the religion, and the culture of so called African Americans. Anyone who understands the tenacity of white supremacy would be crazy to believe that they would not try to control their diets as well. For years, black Americans associated "slave food" with culture food and called it "soul food." We were not eating "soul food" prior to slavery. We had our own diets. Black American slaves however, had to eat whatever they had to due to the lack of food. Once we were freed we had lost all knowledge of what we used to eat. Dr. Llaila Afrika, a prominent holistic doctor declared that European diets are aiding in the killing of black America. He questioned why black Americans suffer the most from diabetes and heart disease and blindness. His answer was clear: "We are eating from European minds and we are out of our mind. That's the problem."

Another holistic doctor who strongly agreed that black Americans needed to change their European diets immediately was Alfredo Darrington Bowman, otherwise known as Dr. Sebi. Dr. Sebi spent a lifetime specifying what foods black people should and should not eat. He lived by the motto, if the human body is electric, which it is, we should only give it electric

---

[19]https://melaninandhoneydotcom.files.wordpress.co m/2016/07/degruy-joy-post-traumatic-slave-syndrome.pdf

food. He also was a world renowned natural healer who helped the lives of many popular entertainers, such as Left-Eye Lopez and Michael Jackson, through proper diet and a healthy lifestyle. Dr. Sebi also claimed to have the cures for, aids, lupus, diabetes and many other diseases. He wanted to tell the nation of his research and findings, but he was denied from making his findings public by mainstream media outlets.

"After curing my thirteenth aids patient, my mother said, 'they're going to get you.'"—Dr. Sebi

Chapter 8: The Perpetual Assault

The hypocrisy of democracy is calling America the land of the free, but never giving the African-American the land to exercise that freedom. The government denied us the necessary tools that we needed to build up our communities while at the same time providing those tools to everyone else. Many European settlers received thousands of acres just for arriving to America. This was purposefully done to keep black people, who were just freed from slavery, disenfranchised. How can you offer thousands of acres of land to a people who have no affiliation with the country over people who have built the country? It was based on race and not nationality. If you had the right color skin, you could always have a shot to win. How can black America ever see this as land of the free? To African-Americans, it is a land of captivity. It is the land of hypocrisy.

Even the great Dr. Martin Luther King Jr. had come to this same conclusion. Just having the right to vote was not enough. There were no resources or land given to black Americans after kidnapping and committing genocide against them. Dr. King is quoted as saying, "I fear I integrated my people in a burning house."[20] He sought out to obtain what had been forgotten and neglected, the reparations. He organized the Poor People's Campaign and he traveled all across

---

[20] https://www.goodreads.com/quotes/7658368-we-have-fought-hard-and-long-for-integration-as-i

the nation bringing up valid points that American educators love to leave out:

At the very same time that America refused to give the Negro any land, through an act of congress our government was giving away millions of acres of land in the West and the Midwest, which meant that it was willing to undergird its white peasants from Europe with an economic floor. But not only did they give the land, they built land grant colleges with government money to teach them how to farm. Not only that, they provided county agents to further their expertise in farming. Not only that, they provided low interest rates in order that they could mechanize their farms. Not only that, today many of these people are receiving millions of dollars in federal subsidies not to farm and they are the very people telling the black man that he ought to lift himself by his own bootstraps. This is what we are faced with and this is a reality. Now, when we come to Washington in this campaign, "we're coming to get our check."[21]

Dr. Martin Luther King Jr. was wide awake and knew exactly what the solution was. It was the unpaid reparations that were promised and never paid that created a domino effect into almost every problem in the black community today. By not paying reparations, this government made sure that we, as a nation of people, would always be dependent on them.

---

[21]https://www.pbs.org/wgbh/pages/frontline/shows/race/etc/script.html

Dr. Martin Luther King Jr. was supposed to lead the Poor People's Campaign in April to the fight for reparations. He was assassinated in that same month of April. White supremacists never cared about voting or integration, they became even richer after segregation because we spent all of our money at their establishments. However, when we started asking for reparations that was seen as act of war.

1990 U.S.A	$1.2 Billion or $20,000 Each	JAPANESE AMERICANS
1990 AUSTRIA	$25 Million to Holocaust Survivors	JEWISH CLAIMS ON AUSTRIA
1988 CANADA	250,000 Sq. Miles of Land	INDIANS & ESKIMOS
1988 CANADA	$230 Million	JAPANESE CANADIANS
1986 U.S.A.	$32 Million 1836 Treaty	OTTAWAS OF MICHIGAN
1985 U.S.A.	$31 Million	CHIPPEWAS OF WISCONSIN
1985 U.S.A.	$12.3 Million	SEMINOLES OF FLORIDA
1985 U.S.A.	$105 Million	SIOUX OF SOUTH DAKOTA
1980 U.S.A.	$81 Million	KLAMATHS OF OREGON
1971 U.S.A.	$1 Billion + 44 Million Acres of Land	ALASKA NATIVES LAND SETTLEMENT
1952 GERMANY	$822 Million to Holocaust Survivors	GERMAN JEWISH SETTLEMENT

[22]

80

As you can see, African-Americans are not on this chart. It is estimated that 14.2 trillion dollars are owed to the descendants of slavery in the US, for the tyranny of white supremacy dating from slavery to Jim Crow (Not including systemic incarceration). No descendant has seen a dollar or an acre. The response has only been cold stares and small head nods. To call this the land of the free when it keeps all the tools for freedom for one nation while depriving another nation seems contradictory. That is freedom for one people and oppression for another. When you oppress people, you don't want them to be free at all. Empty apologies don't matter one damn bit if it's not followed by action. People who are oppressive want the people they are oppressing to be in an inferior position and it is the actions or lack of action that proves it. The best apology an oppressor can give is stop oppressing which means giving back what you stole and that's exactly what this nation refuses to do. It's not just mere words of acknowledgement, but it must involve action or it is clearly in vain. Furthermore, if it is not met with action, to the ears of the oppressed it sounds like a clear case of insanity. It's insanity for people to want to build statues of people who wanted to uphold slavery. It's insanity to consider yourself a Nobel academic institution when you were started by the donations profited from slavery. It's insanity to think it's not a perpetual crime to inherit the profits gained from the stolen labor from another nation of people.

---

[22]http://xroads.virginia.edu/~UG03/johnson/public_ht ml/Soc410/chart.html

The most appalling aspect of slavery was that some former slave masters, unlike the people they were enslaving, received reparations from the government. Slave masters got up to three-hundred dollars per slave out of compassion because the government knew how difficult it must have been for them to have to release their property, my ancestors. Knowing that one detail alone, reality sets in. America paints a very clear picture that it wishes to keep so called African-Americans in an inferior position. However, one thing is for certain, it would be quite dangerous to try keeping a people in an inferior position if God holds them in a superior position. That would be declaring war on God himself. There is only one problem with that, man has never and will never have the capabilities to declare war on God. So while at times, he may appear to be winning in own eyes, in the eyes of God, his efforts are futile and he is only condemning himself. If so called African-Americans are the descendants of the Igbo tribe, who were documented to be captured the most during the transatlantic slave trade, then they are the descendants of the ancient Israelites. Consequently, that would mean America has not been oppressing some "regular black folk," that would mean America (as Egypt, Babylon, Assyria, Persia, Greece, and Rome), enslaved the very Chosen People of God.

So it would seem that the relationship between black and white Americans is dependent on one word, reparations. Without reparations, the relationship has not been amended. One thing is for certain, empty apologies do not heal the atrocities of slavery and Jim

Crow. For example, you cannot steal my car and leave me walking, and then when you see me walking, you want to make peace while you're still in my car. That's illogical. Give me my car back and then we can talk about having peace between us. In fact, more should be given just for causing me the trouble, but never mind that, just give back what you stole. White Americans generally feel uncomfortable at this point of the conversation. If they are uncomfortable hearing this truth, imagine how uncomfortable black Americans are living this truth.

The issue of unpaid reparations has to be seriously discussed again because after the civil rights movement, it was perceived that equality had finally been granted to black Americans, which is until black businesses started closing by the thousands. We would see that after we were allowed to eat in white establishments, black business owners started going out of business. Instead of driving in the black taxis, black people chose to ride in the white taxis. Instead of staying at the black-owned motels and hotels, black people chose to stay at the white hotels.

The great decrease in black businesses ultimately caused a huge decline in the black economy as well. Some people argue that the civil rights act was allowed because white people understood the spending power of black communities. With no reparations given and no practice of group economics, it was only a matter of time before black communities would be on the decline. Black people could shop at white stores, black people could eat at white restaurants, and black people could go to white schools and that's where the greatest mistake was made. We allowed people who hated us to educate our children on history. It would be in the schools, and more specifically the history classrooms, that the greatest crime would take place.

"We're coming for the check." –Dr. Martin Luther King

Chapter 9: Still Denying History

In the beginning of school, they teach you history. However, after gaining just a small amount of consciousness, you begin to realize something. History is a lie and Europeans control the narrative to that lie. The narrative starts with God. What a privilege it must be for a white child in America to see an image of God and every image of God looks like someone in their family, or to see all the little angels around God and all the angels look like someone in their family. The thought about how this might affect black children is not even considered. Black Americans never see a divine image of themselves and that is because white supremacy rules the social structure of America. It does not stop there. American education teaches you about the great philosophers of Greece, the great intellectuals of Rome, and all the Kings and Queens and Dukes of Europe. They even teach about the history of great Chinese empires and other Asian kingdoms. That instills a sense of pride in young European and Asian Americans from an early age. It gives them a sense of worth and a sense of identity.

What about black Americans though? They took the chains off our body and they put them on our minds by omitting history and lying about history. They teach that the beginning of our history started with the lash of the whip on the slave plantations. To further the abuse, white Americans act as if black Americans should be a little grateful for slavery because they got "religion" out of it. This is wrong.

This is criminal. No nation on the earth began their existence as slaves, yet that's exactly what America teaches by ignoring history prior to Trans-Atlantic Slave Trade. The fact is that American education is structured to be convenient for white children. By not teaching white children about the great West African kingdoms that existed prior to the Transatlantic Slave Trade, America is conditioning white children and black children to be willfully ignorant of black history and black culture.

When you steal a people and hide their history from them, you are trying to control them; you are trying to dehumanize them. It has always been white supremacy's goal to dehumanize black Americans. This was done so that the majority of white people would not feel bad about committing genocide and enslaving them. This type of thinking still exists today. Dr. Joy Degruy described it as cognitive dissonance. It's when someone creates a false ideology in order to not distort what they perceive to be reality. If white children do not have to learn about West African kingdoms, then it must not be important. Furthermore, if that society is not important, then the people who made that society is not important, despite the fact that the descendants of those people are right there in the same classroom as white students. So therefore, it's perceived that black Americans have never contributed anything to the world until white Europeans had us in chains. This type of educating is purposefully conditioning white students to feel superior and black students to feel inferior. I personally believe no one is born a racist. White supremacy is a learned behavior in American society, and the American educational system, by omitting black history, aids in that behavior.

What do black children learn in school? The false idea that our kingdoms in West Africa were of no importance. We learn that our ancestors prior to slavery must not have been important at all, since our white educators never teach about them. They want us to think that we come from nothing because they want us to feel insignificant. History prior to slavery must be taught regularly, in order not to perpetuate ignorance. Are African-Americans supposed to view America as the land of the free when America still hides their history? "How Sway?" That notion of freedom becomes a lie if you take the physical chains off, but you leave the mental chains on. If you can control the history of a people, you can control the future of that people. By controlling and distorting history, white supremacy is able to travel freely through public schools—invisible and unnoticed. When this is done, there's no need for a white man in a white hood to ride around burning torches. He doesn't have to do that when black children are being taught that their history begins with slavery. That is terror enough.

The American education system has not just distorted black American history, it has left large parts out. These details would change the way black Americans saw themselves and how other cultures saw black Americans and that was a threat to white supremacy. They teach that every black American ancestor came to America on slave ships. However, it would turn out, that also was a lie. One brother who understood that lie completely was Dr. Ivan Sertima.

He was an author and he asserted in his book, *They Came before Columbus*, that black people had existed in America way before Europeans traveled here. That immediately causes cognitive dissonance within white Americans, because most believe Christopher Columbus actually discovered America. That's obviously a lie. He found a nation that was inhabited with aboriginal peoples and immediately begin to commit genocide and enslave them. In Columbus' diary he wrote about his first trip to the Americas: *The Indians are so naive and so free with their possessions that no one who has not witnessed them would believe it. When you ask for something they have, they never say, 'no,'...To the contrary, they offer to share with anyone...They would make fine servants...With fifty men, we could subjugate them all and make them do whatever we want.*[23]

He would follow through with his plan and commit huge amounts of genocide on aboriginal Americans. This man is considered a hero in America, however, he was one of the biggest terrorists that the world has ever known. Dr. Ivan Sertima's book goes into great detail about some of the atrocities committed by Columbus and other European leaders onto the aboriginals. His claim that black Americans did not all come from West Africa on slave ships was ground shaking and unheard of.

---

[23] Columbus, Christopher, and Clements R. Markham. "Journal of the First Voyage of Columbus." *The Journal of Christopher Columbus (During His First Voyage, 1492-93)*

That is until a famous white reporter by the name of Glenn Beck did a report on some ancient Native American artifacts. He did a report about a stone that was found in Ohio in 1860. The stones existed years before any Europeans had come to America. On the stones were the Ten Commandments, written in an ancient form of block Hebrew. Ironically, they found an identical stone in Israel in 1900. Geologists at the time said that both cases were just hoaxes. Nevertheless, one fact about Israel is, it was once considered North East Africa before the building of the Suez Canal. Whoever made the stones in Ohio had to have some connection to the people that were in ancient Israel. Glenn Beck had one simple question as he looked into the camera while doing the report, "Why haven't we been taught about this?"

It's good to know that some white people, such as Jane Elliot, challenge white supremacy and the education system in America, but the number is far too few. As mentioned earlier, one remark white supremacists love to say to black people is, "your own people sold you into slavery." This has been one of the most ignorant statements that white supremacy has ever concocted. No brother sells his brother into slavery, only a fool would believe that. Are Chinese people and Japanese people the same people just because they have similar skin color? No. Are Russians and Englishmen the same just because they have similar skin color? No. See how crazy this sounds? So why would someone believe all black people are the same just because they have the same skin color? The local tribes did not sell each other to Europeans. They sold black people that looked like them, but were not them and not of the same tribe as them. They sold black people who were migrators onto their land. The main group of people that was sold in the Transatlantic Slave Trade was the Igbo tribe.

The Igbo tribe is and have always been self-sufficient people who mainly reside in Nigeria today. If you ask any Igbo person, they will tell you that Nigeria is not their homeland at all. They migrated there from Israel. The Igbo tribe is indeed the descendants of the Israelites of Ancient Israel and it's even be proven by DNA. The word Igbo is a derivative of Heebo and Heebo is a derivative of Hebrew. The corruption of the word Hebrew, Heebo, and Igbo is explained in great detail in the book, "IBOS: Hebrew Exiles from Israel". Per Professor David Eltis and Professor David Richardson in *Atlas of the Trans-Atlantic Slave Trade*:

The British were the major buyers before they banned their own slave traffic in 1807. They were replaced by the Portuguese and Spanish for as long as the traffic continued here. The majority of the captives were speakers of Igbo dialect.[24]

If you take religion away from the Bible, it just becomes a history book of the Israelites. A white European Rabbi by the name of Yehudah Ben Shomeyr once made a huge proclamation on live radio. He said the Transatlantic Slave Trade is connected to Deuteronomy 28 in the Bible. He went on to say that the majority of slaves who were brought to the Caribbean islands and to the Americas were of Hebrew lineage. He said that the prophecy of the Israelites in Deuteronomy 28 matched perfectly with the history of so called "African-Americans." Israelites were prophesied to go into slavery again by ships. African-Americans went into slavery by ships. Israelites were prophesied to lose their name. African-Americans lost their name. Israelites were prophesied to lose their land. African-Americans lost their land. Israelites were prophesied to lose their culture. African-Americans lost their culture.

The tribes are lost, but they are not dead. They are lost because they have no self-identity because it was taken from them in captivity. They are lost because they are spread out. They are lost because

---

[24] "Atlas of the Transatlantic Slave Trade." *Politics of Everyday Life | Yale University Press*, 16 Feb. 2015, yalebooks.yale.edu/book/9780300212549/atlas-transatlantic-slave-trade. 127.

they have no knowledge of their original names, history, or culture. Rabbi Yehudah Ben Shomeyr, a White European Jew, said that African-Americans, like most slaves involved in the Transatlantic Slave Trade, were of the Igbo tribe meaning they were of the lost tribes of Israel. Was this the reason why African-American history has yet to be revealed? Is this why nothing about African-American history is revealed before the 1600s? If the American education system taught black history prior to the 1600s, it would be obvious that African-Americans were of the Igbo tribe and they were sold into slavery by local African tribes to Europeans. However, the unraveling would not stop there. People would read more about the history of the Igbo tribe and understand that they are factually proven to be the descendants of the lost tribes of Israel. On the flip side of that, white America would also have to face the fact that the black aboriginals of America also had ties to Hebrew heritage as well. This means white Americans did not just enslave and commit genocide against some regular black people from Africa, despite the propaganda that they constantly promote. More specifically, that means America enslaved and committed genocide against the very group that they see as God's Chosen People. Since the African-American connection with the Igbo tribe is real, then that means America enslaved Israelites and gave them new names such as "niggers, Negroes, colored people, blacks, and African-Americans." Now if this truth ever reached the masses of society, it would cause quite a bit of cognitive dissonance to say the least. It definitely would make sense why they don't teach about it. It cannot be a coincidence that African-American history and the history and prophecies of the Israelites match up perfectly. That's why white supremacy would rather start black history with picking cotton. Perpetuating the lie is comfortable, but acknowledging the truth is too much for them to bear.

"Indeed I tremble for my country when I reflect that God is just: that his justice cannot sleep forever"
–Thomas Jefferson

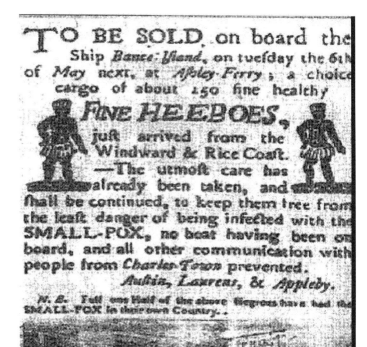

TO BE SOLD, on board the Ship *Bance-Island*, on tuesday the 6th of *May* next, at *Ashley-Ferry*; a choice cargo of about 250 fine healthy FINE HEEBOES, just arrived from the Windward & Rice Coast. —The utmost care has already been taken, and shall be continued, to keep them free from the least danger of being infected with the SMALL-POX, no boat having been on board, and all other communication with people from *Charles-Town* prevented.

Austin, Laurens, & Appleby.

N. B. Full one half of the above Negroes have had the SMALL-POX in their own Country.

Chapter 10: Still Denying Culture

White supremacists just love to give their opinion on how "good negroes" should look and behave. Black masculinity was not to be accepted as it was viewed as a threat. In the past, we were supposed to know our place. "Knowing your place" was code for black people to quiver in the sight of white people and do their bidding at any given time. They wanted black masculinity eliminated and they wanted that natural black warrior spirit to die. Well, you can't turn warriors into feeble people overnight. That takes time. That is a process. For centuries, all knowledge of African-American culture would be suppressed by the United States government. From slavery, to Jim Crow, to systemic mass incarceration, it has been white supremacy's biggest priority to control what black culture is and is not.

One must remember in the days of Marcus Garvey, Malcolm X, and Dr. Martin Luther King Jr., black people dressed very dignified and noble. Black men wore suits daily, not just on Sunday morning. They had a sense of class and style that surely enraged the white society who had recently had them confined to chains only a few decades prior. The term "uppity negro" would be used to refer to any black person who had any self-respect or self-love. If a black man wanted land, he would be considered an "uppity negro." If a black man wanted his own business, he would be considered an "uppity negro". If a black man wanted to enjoy life as white people did with the same securities, he would be considered an "uppity negro." The insanity of white supremacy is indeed never ending.

Dignified black people were too much for white supremacists to bear. Hidden powers came together and decided, they needed to change the culture of black America drastically. What better way to do that than through what they love the most? Music and television. White supremacy knew that through television, if they fed us false images of ourselves, we would inevitably transform into those images. It wasn't enough that they murdered and deported our leaders. Right after the political assault in the 60s, white supremacists began their moral attack in the 70s. They initiated psychological warfare on the very culture of black Americans. In the 1970s, we would see wave after wave of "pimp and ho" movies, exploiting black women and stereotyping black men. Every year it would get worse. There were so many blockbuster movies about black men disrespecting black women, you would have thought in order to be a black American man, you had to be a pimp at least once in your life.

One detail that many older black people will attest to is that black families (pre-civil rights) were together. Divorce in the black family was hardly heard of. However, after civil rights, black marriages ended more so than ever before. Surely, the incredible amount of negative movies had to play a part in that. Not to mention it was white production companies signing black artists to portray such negative roles. The same would be the case in the 80s and the 90s. After the "pimp and prostitute" era, the black community would be bombed with yet another propaganda pattern. Gangsta and thugs. White people would make billions off of black gangsta movies, promoting the idea that all black men were dangerous and criminals and black women were loud and had attitudes. Are we to think that propaganda did not have a connection to mass incarceration? Of course it did. Hip-hop would be one of the main tools for this. What had begun as positive and conscious became dark and rough. Who was usually getting paid to promote the negativity in hip-hop? Some old white man in a suit, just being honest. One mainstream rapper is quoted in saying that he once had written an amazing song that was conscious and uplifting. He said he played it for his white executives at the record label he was signed to. After hearing it, the white executive said, "It's no good man, you need to say "Niggas" some more."

Our music culture was attacked by white supremacy and our cultural food was attacked by white supremacy. We must understand who we were prior to being enslaved. Once we know how we lived, and what we ate, we will return to our natural states. We must all admit that white supremacy's goal is to make black people either more like white people or obsolete altogether. Neither must be allowed. This is incredibly obvious when it comes to diet. Black Americans have to get off of European diets. The food chart that we grew up on was promoted by dairy companies for a reason, to make money. How can pig be in a food chart? Like Really? We wonder why we are leading the nation in heart disease and diabetes; it's because of the food. How can black people who have no history of cancer in their family and who have never smoked or drink still get cancer in their body? It's the food. We are eating like we are Europeans, but we are not the same people. Polar bears do not have the same diets as grizzly bears, so why do we think people from different climates and regions are supposed to eat the same? We had our own diets and our own culture. That's why it's so important to know your original culture, despite the fact that American education teaches you to ignore it. When you practice your culture, you are truly being yourself. There is a natural peace that comes with that. We should strive to be who God intended us to be, rather than what white people think we should be.

Chapter 11: Creating Self-Hatred

African-Americans have been totally stripped of everything. Our history, our culture, and even our names were stripped from us. During slavery, even the African drum was outlawed in America. Many brothers and sisters today love music for one reason, the bass. The booming of the drums has always been a part of our culture. The pounding of the drum is spiritual for so called African-Americans. It was used in many slave revolts. This powerful sound put fear in the face of white plantation owners all across the nation. After a while, it was outlawed in hope of keeping black people meek and docile. This was their way of brainwashing us. They wanted to turn "revolutionary negroes," into "good negroes." Please understand, in the eyes of white supremacy, a good Negro is a self-hating Negro. "Good negroes" don't ruffle any feathers. "Good Negroes" don't ask any questions. Make no mistake about it; although white supremacy might hate black people, they love "good negroes."

Dr. Edward Robinson once said, "Race esteem is the foundation of self-esteem. Race esteem is the flower and self-esteem is the essence to that flower."[25] These wise words imply that if a people have no knowledge of who they are, they also will have no self-respect or self-love for each other, which creates self-hatred and hatred for one another. However, it won't be just a lack of self-love and self-respect

---

[25] Robinson, Edward. "African Genesis."

within that people only, but other nations around that people will also look at them with a lack of respect as well. This government knew that and slavery was evident of that. In order to put the chains around the necks of black children, white supremacists would have to condition the masses to neither love nor respect black people. They had to make it appear that little black children were not humans at all, but just merely farm animals.

America made it clear that no black person was entitled to any respect from a white person. Rather than respecting us, they used all of their time and energy to vilify us. They even used the English language to vilify black people. White supremacy, through massive false propaganda and media made the world think black is synonymous with ugly and vile. Europeans associated the color black with everything evil and negative: Black head; Black hole; Blackmail; Blackleg; Blackball; Black mark. This was and is the everyday language of Europeans. If a child, black or white, continues to hear the color black being associated with everything bad and evil, how is he or she going to feel when she comes in contact with a black man or black woman? The very English language conditions white people to be racist and conditions victims of racism to self-hate themselves.

Around 1805, white supremacy begins to spread the false propaganda that African-Americans came from the jungle. That was also a lie. They would then produce "Tarzan" movies to further promote that lie. Yet, they would never teach African-Americans about the beautiful kingdoms we came from in West Africa. There would be no mention of Mansa Musa. There would be no mention of the Songhai Empire. There would be no mention of the Slave Coast on the Negroland map also known as the Kingdom of Judah. There would be no mention that black people were in America prior to the Transatlantic Slave Trade. Still to this day, most of us have no knowledge of our original names, language, land, or culture, but we are free? After they stripped us of all that we were, they said we were free. We were free, but we were only freed when white supremacy knew that we were a completely broken people. We were not destroyed physically, but we had been totally destroyed mentally.

Most white Americans have the privilege of ignoring such frustrations. This silence has been the main reason why less and less black people even care to have the conversation of racism with white people any longer. It becomes incredibly exhausting, pleading for the same things over and over. There is nothing else that can be said that our conscious scholars from our communities haven't already explained. All the information and the data is available to everyone, but many choose to ignore it. Unfortunately, black people do not have that luxury. For black people, we must understand that once white supremacy took the chains off our feet, they put them on our mind. We were only freed once they knew we were completely brainwashed.

"There's no excuse for the young people not knowing who the heroes and heroines are or were." – Nina Simone

Chapter 12: Final Summary

There is no book that could fill up all the atrocities that white supremacy has placed upon black America. Nevertheless, one thing is clear; the American dream has been the black American nightmare. The American dream has become a facade for black America, a perpetuating contradiction in a never-ending hypocrisy. Black Americans have tried profusely to live with white Americans peacefully. If you look at the assault on black communities, you would think it was black Americans who enslaved white Americans. But no, it was white Americans who kidnapped and enslaved black Americans. Black people have tried holding hands with white people, they have tried singing gospel songs with white people, and they have tried praying with white people. Nothing changes however, except the prison population, which constantly increases with black attendance.

White supremacy promotes the idea that this is because of "black on black crime." On the contrary, the research is out now, and it has been concluded by many scholars that the root of black on black crime is white on black crime. Getting black people to commit crimes on one another has always been a goal of white supremacy. America has been teaching self-hate through mainstream media and orchestrating the destruction of black communities to grow the prison population since the days of Nixon.

The American government under the shadow of white supremacy has committed genocide against so-called African-Americans and still is today. They enslaved them, raped them, lynched them, freed them and locked them up again. No reparations have ever been issued. How can someone with a "healthy" conscious think this doesn't deserve reparations? People that ignore this are ignoring the greatest injustice the world has ever known. The failure to highlight the fact that Dr. Martin Luther King Jr. was assassinated just days before he was going to fight for reparations is indeed appalling. This loud silence toward the answer to improving black communities has become so overwhelming, that the black community cannot differentiate who in the white community is a friend and who is a foe. I have a way to make it clear for you. The good white friends of the black community are the ones fighting for the unpaid reparations of the descendants of slaves. Everybody else is everybody else. That seems fair, lest we continue to believe that this is the land of the free while it is in fact for black Americans, the land of captivity. It's the ultimate illusion of inclusion.

Some of the brightest scholars, educated by white institutions, such as Dr. Na'im Akbar and Randal Robinson agree that the attack on the nation of black America has been unjustified and never compensated. Black Americans are constantly dared to speak about these issues because white supremacy is still alive and well today. We are dared to speak about real black history and our oppression by white America. We are dared to research whatever relationship we may have with the people of ancient Israel. It cannot be by chance that aboriginal Americans had the Ten Commandments written in ancient Hebrew. It cannot be by chance that the most sought out people in the

Transatlantic Slave Trade were of the Igbo Tribe, the descendants of ancient Israel. It cannot be by chance that slaves who built the First African Baptist Church carved Hebrew words in the seats before they could read and write in English.

We are dared to speak up for group economics and black love. This has to stop and we cannot let our white jobs or white constituents ever make us hesitate from speaking truth. Those days are over. If I was employed by white people, I would not be allowed to write such a book as this. That is because when you work for white America, there are some truths you cannot speak about, no matter the occupation. If one cannot speak truth at all times, especially when it concerns threats to humanity, then that person is on some form of plantation and must seek freedom at some point.

It comes down to this. African-Americans didn't seek to build a new world off the backs of slaves, Europeans did. African-Americans didn't offer forty acres and a mule for the atrocities of slavery and then blatantly ignore them, Europeans did. White America knew that if they never gave the reparations, there would always be an imbalance in power. This made black Americans totally dependent on the resources of white America. They made us into a nation of consumers. Anyone who understands business a little bit understands that it is the producer who wills the true power. Therefore, the answer becomes clear, the solution for black Americans is reparation or maybe complete separation, at least when it comes to finances if not entirely. To even speak about reparation in America is considered somewhat taboo. Well if it's taboo for white people to talk about reparation, it should be taboo for black people to spend money on white businesses. What needs to be corrected is what has been neglected. One cannot correct what they fail to even acknowledge.

Until we are organized enough to go obtain our rightfully owed reparations, black America should spend 100% of their time mastering group economics as Black Wall Street did. Any average American citizen would agree black people shop at every other business, but their own. As it was emphasized in the first chapter, Black people will shop at white businesses. Black people shop at Asian businesses. Black people shop at Indian businesses. However, which one of the groups is going out of their way supporting black businesses? It seems to the author that other culture groups support their businesses without thinking twice, while black people have to beg and convince each other to support black businesses. This should not be the case at all. Why do white people overly support white businesses? Why do Asian people overly support Asian business? Why do Indian people overly support Indian businesses? Because they love their community. Group economics is a matter of self-love and love for your community which is love for your nation. Black America has to wake up and realize that we have one of the biggest spending powers in the world. Yet, we give the majority of that money to the descendants of the people who enslaved us. This makes no sense. Group economics is a matter of survival. The base of group economics is owning businesses and having trade skills. I am not saying to not fight for degrees. However once again, most people will agree, in the real world, it's the person who has the degree who usually works for the person who owns a trade. Diplomas and trades must be seen as equally as important. However, it must be clearly understood, a person who has a trade will never be out of work.

Once we understand all of this, we can save ourselves. When we love the idea of shopping with black businesses as much as we love clubbing, we will save ourselves. When we learn how to build houses as easily as we learn how to dribble a ball, we will save ourselves. When we enjoy making clothes just as much as we love dancing, we will save ourselves. When we learn how to grow food, like we learn how to play video games, we will save ourselves. With reparations and restitution or just by mastering group economics, we can save ourselves. We can save ourselves by finishing the work of Marcus Garvey, Malcolm X, and Dr. King. When that is done, we will reach that promise land that Dr. Martin Luther King Jr. spoke about in his last speech. If God is a just God, and He is, nothing will stop us from reaching it—not even this hypocrisy disguised as a democracy.

Notes

.

Made in the USA
Columbia, SC
27 November 2024

47637846R00067